T0173824

Wharfie Animator

Focus Animation

Series Editor:
Giannalberto Bendazzi

The Focus Animation Series aims to provide unique, accessible content that may not otherwise be published. We allow researchers, academics, and professionals the ability to quickly publish high impact, current literature in the field of animation for a global audience.

This series is a fine complement to the existing, robust animation titles available through CRC Press/Focal Press.

Currently an independent scholar, is a former Visiting Professor of History of Animation at the Nanyang Technological University in Singapore and a former professor at the Università degli Studi di Milano. We welcome any submissions to help grow the wonderful content we are striving to provide to the animation community: giannalbertobendazzi@gmail.com.

Twice the First: Quirino Cristiani and the Animated
Feature Film
Giannalberto Bendazzi

Floating Worlds: A Short History of Japanese Animation
Maria Roberta Novielli

Redesigning Animation United Productions of America
Cinzia Bottini

Puppetry, Puppet Animation and the Digital Age
Rolf Giesen

Infinite Animation: The Life and Work of Adam Beckett
Pamela Taylor Turner

Václav Trojan: Music Composition in Czech Animated Films
Marco Bellano

WHARFIE ANIMATOR

Harry Reade, The Sydney Waterfront, and the Cuban Revolution

Max Bannah

CRC Press
Taylor & Francis Group
Boca Raton London New York

CRC Press is an imprint of the
Taylor & Francis Group, an **informa** business

A FOCAL PRESS BOOK

first edition published 2021
by CRC Press
6000 Broken Sound Parkway NW, Suite 300,
Boca Raton, FL 33487-2742

and by CRC Press
2 Park Square, Milton Park, Abingdon, Oxon, OX14 4RN

© 2021 Taylor & Francis Group, LLC
CRC Press is an imprint of Taylor & Francis Group, LLC

ISBN: 978-0-367-63953-2 (hbk)
ISBN: 978-0-367-63958-7 (pbk)
ISBN: 978-1-003-12149-7 (ebk)

Typeset in Minion Pro
by KnowledgeWorks Global Ltd.

For Juan Padrón
(29 January 1947–24 March 2020)

Contents

Acknowledgements

THIS BOOK IS DERIVED from a Master of Arts (Research) thesis written at the Queensland University of Technology (QUT) in 2007. It would have remained unpublished if not for animation scholar Giannalberto Bendazzi's surprise invitation to include it in CRC Press' Focus Animation series. I cannot thank him enough. I also owe thanks to the QUT Creative Industries academic and library staff, particularly Dr. Mark Pennings and Dr. Andrew McNamara for encouraging my interest in animation studies.

Much of the material in this book has been made possible by people who were kind enough to share their memories of Harry Reade with me. Sincere thanks go to filmmakers Norma Disher and Jock Levy, former wharfie and artist Clem Millward, journalists David and Pat Evans, journalist and commentator Paddy McGuinness, animators Juan Padrón and Hernán Henriquez, comic-strip artist Juan López Fernández (aka JAN), animated cinema historian Willema Wong Tejeda and documentary filmmaker Harry Tanner, for their willing and generous contributions. Special thanks to the late premier Cuban animator Juan Padrón for introducing me to the fascinating life of Harry Reade in 1982, and to the caretaker of Reade's estate Pat Evans for granting me access to his creative works and unpublished autobiography. Also, thanks go to veteran animators, Alex Stitt, Bruce Petty and Anne Joliffe who offered their recollections of Australian animation during the 1950s.

I should also like to thank staff in the following institutions who provided assistance and invaluable documents: the Australian Security Intelligence Organisation (ASIO), the Maritime Union of Australia, the Australian National Maritime Museum, the National Film and Sound Archive of Australia, the Cuban Institute of the Art and Industry of Cinema (Instituto Cubano de Arte y Industria Cinematográficos) and the Fryer Library.

Finally, I especially want to thank my wife Sylvia, who has supported my interest in animation; been civil to eccentric colleagues I've invited to dinner; provided helpful feedback on my work; and kept me awake at night thinking about the use of commas.

About the Author

Max Bannah (b. 1947) lives on Queensland's Sunshine Coast. After studying architecture at the University of Queensland and filmmaking at the London Film School, between 1976 and 2010, he operated a small studio in Brisbane producing illustrations and animation for television commercials and short films. He also lectured in animation at Queensland College of Art Griffith University and at Queensland University of Technology where, in 2007, he completed a Masters by Research degree. He has a particular interest in regional creative practice which is often overlooked in histories that emanate from established centres of cultural activity.

Introduction

IN 1982, I ATTENDED the Fifth World Festival of Animated Films in Zagreb. Six years earlier, I had begun working as a lone practitioner in Brisbane, making a living and supporting a family by animating advertising commercials. At the time, I was one of only a few people working locally in animation and was craving contact with other people actively involved with the medium. My part of the world was a long way from the major centres of animation activity, and prior to the internet, apart from relocating geographically, one way of connecting with an international community was through participation in animation festivals. So, deciding that the production of personal short films might help me escape the moral dilemmas of commercial work as well as link me with other animators, I produced a 4-minute animated film, *Violet and Brutal*, which was accepted for screening in the debut category at the Zagreb festival.

Festivals are wonderful places to discover the like-minded and like-minded wannabes, and accordingly at Zagreb I met many warm, humble and highly acclaimed practitioners who all shared a common interest in the films being screened. One evening in the guest hotel, I got talking with Juan Padrón, the celebrated Cuban animation artist. We communicated through a form of mangled 'Spanglish', and when necessary clarified uncertainties with drawings on beer-coasters. At some point Juan asked if I knew of an Australian, Harry Reade, who had taught him animation skills in Cuba during the 1960s. I had never heard of him but was intrigued that such a person had emerged from the conservative

Cold War climate of Robert Menzies' Australia to have a cultural impact in Cuba. At the time, the commercial orientation of mainstream Australian animation practice was diametrically opposed to the ideological imperatives of a socialist revolution. Juan's mentor, therefore, seemed to be an anomaly. Who was Harry Reade? What was his involvement with animation in both Australia and Cuba, and how and why had a little known animator moved between two worlds that were so different?

Before the night was over, Juan did a drawing in my notebook. It depicted a vampire character from his animated short-film, *Filminuto No. 1* (1982), which had also screened at the Festival. In the drawing, the character enquires of a second vampire, 'Hello! Are you a bloody vampire from…?' Wearing a broad-brimmed hat with dangling corks, the iconic device associated with chasing flies off the face of an Australian swagman, the second figure replies, 'Bloody Australia, mate'. The image is a whimsical statement about the way in which similarities outweigh the differences between two strangers but the pun on the word 'bloody' in the voice bubbles also affirmed that Padrón was familiar with commonly used Australian idioms.

Fourteen years later, I read an item in the Brisbane Courier-Mail about a former revolutionary called Harry Reade who was repairing his self-made boat in the Great Sandy Strait on the Queensland coast. The piece prompted me to check my notebook for confirmation that after all that time I was reading about Juan Padrón's incongruous mentor. In the article, Reade reminisced about his contribution to Cuban animation while also expressing a direct and uncompromising personal approach to life:

> Mr Reade is glad he had the chance to play a small part in Cuba's transformation, and he is still remembered for his creation of animated cartoon propaganda character 'Pepe' who taught the Cubans everything from first aid to permaculture. He is a recognized 'fundedor' (founder) of Cuba's animated cartoon industry. Not for him the froth and bubble of Barbara Cartland and Dad and Dave

writing. 'You've got to reach for the stars, try to change things. Man has but one life to live and, to me the greatest of all causes is the liberation of humanity. I was lucky to be around people who did it (in Cuba)'.

(Green, G. 1996)

FIGURE 0.1 Notebook sketch by Juan Padrón, Zagreb, 1982. (Author's personal collection.)

By this time, my solitary professional circumstances in Brisbane had changed. A small but growing animation community of students, academics, enthusiasts and practitioners had led to the formation of Queensland Animators Group (QAG), which aimed to provide an environment for those with an interest in the medium to meet and promote the production, appreciation and potential of the animation arts. QAG received modest funding from Film Queensland for administrative purposes and support for an informal series of presentations by national and international animation luminaries. It was agreed that Reade would make an ideal addition to the series because he was a little-known, marginal character who had done something out of the ordinary.

So I went looking for him and more than a year later finally tracked him down to a caravan park in the small coastal township of Boonaroo. After I sent him an introductory letter, he agreed to present a public lecture at the State Library of Queensland. But when I suggested he focus on animation—how he'd got involved, what he'd produced and why—I detected an anarchic and abrasive tone in his reply. He insisted that during his life he had been involved with many things other than animation. 'I know what I'll talk about. Don't tell me what to say!' We settled on a date, and I posted him a return train ticket and booked a room for him in a comfortable motel.

I had no trouble recognising our guest from the newspaper photo when he got off the train at Roma Street Station. He was wearing old clothes, carried a well-used shopping bag and looked timeworn, rough, tough and unconcerned with appearance. He shook my hand firmly but caught me off-guard when he recited a few lines of poetry and then grunted, 'Name the poem and the poet!' As soon as it registered with him that I was lost, he tightened his grip and said, 'A man oughta flatten you now! It's Lawson's "Faces in the Street"'. An inauspicious start on my part!

I took him home to meet my family, and over dinner he continued his edgy behaviour by dominating the conversation with philosophical quotes, the concerns of disadvantaged aboriginal communities and difficulties facing the resistance movement in East Timor. There was little room for the input of others until he unexpectedly put one of our teenage sons on the spot by challenging him to express an opinion on homosexuality. Given that Harry had spent much of the meal espousing support for marginalised groups, it came as a shock when our son's positive and tolerant response was met with a blistering homophobic tirade. Although just as quickly he calmed down and moved on to other topics, the sudden outburst was difficult to comprehend.

Later in the evening when he stepped up to present his lecture, he maintained the unsettling presence of a stand-and-deliver boxer. From the outset, he spoke with conviction and passion—emphasising ideological slogans and punching the air with a clenched fist. He made it clear he was not interested in illusion, box office returns or the production of banal animation for entertainment—'there were plenty of others who did that stuff well enough'. Instead, he stressed he was driven by an urge to confront the system, promote a political point of view and seek partners in dissent.

Of course, he dismissed the few themes I had suggested and, in their place, presented a distillation of the defining moments that constituted an unusual life. He spoke very little about the process of animation but quite a lot about the social responsibility of artists to critique and reflect on the status quo in order to stimulate radical action in society. It was apparent that his creative experience had been forged from a rough, colourful and intense life—one that had navigated ideological conflicts to promote social change. The relevance of his animation work could only be appreciated in a context linking it to his ferment of experiences, his ideological orientation and the time and places in which he'd lived.

Over drinks at the conclusion of the talk, most agreed they had experienced an unusual but riveting performance. It had broadened their understanding of the diversity of animation practice in Australia during the 1950s, but, more importantly, it had demonstrated the value of individuals and their capacity to assert versions of identity other than those embraced by popular culture or recorded histories. His work had contributed to the creation of an alternative framework through which political, social and cultural themes that marked the 1950s in Australia and the 1960s in Cuba, could be thought about.

Harry mixed with his audience and, knowing he was at the centre of attention, kept up a seemingly jovial but reckless form of provocation. The night ended when I foolishly introduced a female friend as a philosophy lecturer. Perhaps the idea that a woman with the potential to question his articles of faith was a red rag he could not ignore. But whatever the cause, he immediately launched into a demeaning attack that continued for as long as it took for the gathering to disperse, and it was left to me to drive him to his accommodation.

When we arrived at the motel room with its city view across the river, he put on a show of rejecting the comfortable bed. 'I grew up sleepin' in ditches. I'll sleep on the bloody floor'. I told him he had choice and could do what he liked, thanked him for his efforts on behalf of QAG and left bewildered that a person who had led such an intriguing and colourful life seemed incapable of controlling aggressive impulses.

Harry returned to the Great Sandy Straits but in November 1997 went to Sydney to celebrate his 70th birthday with old friends. While there, he was diagnosed with an advanced form of cancer and discovered he was dying. Despite the rheumatism in his hands, he immediately set out to write the second volume of his autobiography (*A Funny Kind of Left-wing Animal*), make a working puppet and design an ecological chookhouse. He made significant advances on the first two tasks and, while working on the third, decided he wanted one last sail on his boat at Boonaroo. On his way back from Sydney, he stayed overnight at our house. My family had braced for his sharp and unpredictable behaviour, but it was clear that he was very sick and had mellowed. There was no sign of the angry old man. This time he was the essence of gentleness, kindness and gratitude. Throughout a restless night and knowing his time was running out, he worked with a sense of urgency on his laptop editing his autobiography. Two weeks after he headed off, I phoned the camping ground to see how he was getting on. He was pleased to hear from me, and when he told me he felt he only had a few days left, I said, 'Harry, I don't really know what to say'. He replied, 'Well, bloody well hang up now, ya wuss!'

Harry Reade died on 7 May 1998, and I regret that I had not recorded his lecture or interviewed him. Years later, I began lecturing at Queensland University of Technology, and feeling the pressure to comply with academic research and publication demands, decided to embark on post-graduate studies. The undertaking once more led me to try to find Harry Reade. The result is this biographical account which examines the forces that shaped Harry and the ways in which he sought to shape his world through the medium of animation.

CHAPTER 1

A Wobbly Road

POLITICAL AND SOCIAL INFLUENCES ON HARRY READE'S EARLY LIFE (1927–1954)

In 1963, the short animated film *La Cosa* (*The Thing*) received Cuba's first international award for animation at the London Film Festival. The award was a boost for Cuban films and vindication of the establishment in 1959 of an animation studio (Dibujos Animados) within the Cuban Institute of the Art and Industry of Cinema (ICAIC). Such international recognition helped to promote a positive image of the Cuban Revolution abroad. Not that ICAIC sought foreign approval. On the contrary, its guiding principle was that foreign recognition would follow if the films were authentic expressions of the Revolution's own needs (Chanan, M. 2004, 131). *La Cosa* is a Marxist parable about the world created by capitalism and the society it sustains, and illustrates how human beings can organise the means of production for their own subsistence. What is intriguing about this film is that it was written and directed by an Australian named Harry Reade—a waterside worker and part-time journalist, author, dramatist, cartoonist, illustrator and animator who linked creative expression with radical action in society.

Although he is a little-known figure in Australian animation history, Harry Reade had an enduring influence on the development of the educational sector of Cuban animation. Given the intense conservatism and anti-communist feeling that prevailed in Australia at the height of the Cold War, how was it that a Sydney wharfie could emerge to have such an impact on revolutionary Cuban culture and society?

Reade recounts the poverty and harshness of his childhood in the first volume of his autobiography, *An Elephant Charging My Chookhouse*—a title prompted by a question that young Harry had asked his father Tom Reade who struggled with what he called 'the bloody system' and his distrust of the world created by capitalism and the society it sustained:

> 'What's capitalism, Dad?'
> 'An elephant charging a chookhouse, shouting, every man for himself!'
>
> (*Reade, H. 1987,* 101)

This personal account of the social reality of Reade's formative years evokes the atmosphere of general hardship experienced by the Australian jobless and their families during the Great Depression. It helps explain his relationship with the society in which he lived and provides an understanding of the intellectual framework guiding his personal development and his identification with working class communities. His story focuses on the conditions that determined his ideological beliefs and his rejection of capitalism.

Reade describes how his mother and father met at Australia's great horse race, the Melbourne Cup. His mother was 18, his father 43: 'He tipped her a wink, bought her a drink, and one thing led to another ... namely my own birth on 17 November 1927 in Murtoa, Victoria' (Reade, H. 1987, 16). His name, Henry Garbutt Reade, honoured his mother, Vera Violet Garbutt, and a nineteenth-century mathematician after whom his father had named himself. Tom Reade had changed his surname from *Reed* to *Reade* in honour of William Winwood Reade who had written *The Martyrdom of Man*—a prominent freethinking text published in 1872, which dealt with four common stages of human development: war, religion, liberty and intellect. William Winwood Reade gave a glimpse of humanity's future by examining the past. He believed science would replace humanity's dependence on religion, and predicted people would be liberated from labour by three inventions: air travel, a fuel to replace coal and oil, and the production of food in factories (Reade, H. 1987, 24).

Harry Reade had been delivered into a world of uncertainty, one in which the speculative euphoria of the Roaring Twenties was turned upside down by the worldwide economic slump of 1929 and the beginning of the Great Depression. With his father out of work, Harry's first memories of childhood were 'bitter sweet recollections of the Hungry Thirties'. By 1930, the rosy glow of romance between his parents had dimmed, and the marriage fell apart. Reade is not certain what contributed to the failure of the relationship but offers that 'theirs was not the only marriage torn apart by the Great Depression. Many marriages were, especially those that were simple unions of the flesh'. His mother left when he was 3, and he never saw her again. He says in his autobiography that because he was so young when she abandoned him, all real knowledge of her was 'denied to memory'. He could not recall the touch of her hand or the colour of her hair, and the only descriptions of her that his father bequeathed him were, 'That's where you got your big nose' on one occasion, and 'Look in the mirror sometime' on another (Reade, H. 1987, 18–32).

Tom Reade, a tough, militant, unemployed and politically committed Wobbly, took on his son's upbringing. He was born in Sydney, in 1883, and became an atheist at the age of 16 when he ran away to sea as a deckhand on a Norwegian barquentine. For a while he worked on the Sydney waterfront before economic recessions and industrial accidents left him unemployed just prior to the World War I. Harry writes of the blustering defiance in his father's character and his 'sign-on' with the Industrial Workers of the World:

> In the early 1900s—young, strong, fearless, penniless and godless—he was ripe for recruitment to the Industrial Workers of the World. The eye double you, double you … the eye, double double you … the 'I Won't Works', the Wobblies. The Wobs. The Reds. They recruited him one Sunday afternoon on the Sydney Domain, with a left hook to the chin.
>
> (Reade, H. 1987, 22)

As a Wobbly, Tom Reade shared the belief that under capitalism any gains or losses made by some workers, from or to bosses, would eventually affect all workers. Therefore, to protect each other, all workers had to support one another in a broader class conflict. The Wobblies were united in their desire to transform capitalist society and pursued the abolition of wage labour and the establishment of an Industrial Commonwealth. They wanted a self-managing society where there were no bosses or 'business agents', and where decisions affecting workers were made by themselves. Their ideological practice centred on the concept of 'direct action' at the work place, 'the point where exploitation was begun'. Direct action encompassed sabotage, go-slow tactics, job control, strikes and every method of waging class war in direct confrontation with the wages system controlled by employers. Frank Farrell describes the general character of the Wobblies in *International Socialism and Australian Labour: The Left in Australia 1919–1939*:

> In terms of worldwide trends the Wobblies were anarcho-syndicalist in that they fused an emotional anarchistic revulsion at organised society with the idea of a giant industrial union emancipating the workers by means of a

general strike and seizure of the means of production. But a dominating aspect of Wobbly agitation was its anarchistic rejection of society, the actual formation of industrial unions being for the most part forgotten.

(Farrell, F. 1981, 14)

Farrell's description of the Wobblies' tendencies did not mean that the Wobblies were Luddites, for they did not engage in industrial sabotage for the sake of it. On the contrary, they 'welcomed mechanisation and demanded it'. However, in a capitalist system, as machines improved and performed the work of people, those same people rather than benefiting from the improved technology by gaining more leisure time were actually working even harder. Reade points out that when he was a child, his father often quoted *The Right to be Lazy,* written in 1883 by the French author, Paul Lafargue (1842–1911) who was a socialist writer and political activist married to Karl Marx's daughter. Lafargue advocated the creation of a political party of the working class. His book urged the working class to reject 'the right to work (the right to be exploited)' as outlined in Tom Paine's, *The Rights of Man* (1791).[1] Lafargue also called on workers to refuse to work more than three hours a day in an attempt to force employers to modernise industry. Such an action, he argued, would assure workers a share of available work and would not take sustenance from other workers in a competitive system. Like *Martyrdom of Man, The Right to be Lazy* too proposed the means for 'people's liberation from labour'.

Reade stresses that while his father campaigned on behalf of the IWW movement, he did not spend his time 'burning down buildings, slugging policemen, selling illegal papers, agitating, and doing time'. As a man looking to feed himself and a child, he had to work (Reade, H. 1987, 29). Like many others jobless during the Depression, his father was down on his luck and took whatever work was at hand: 'fencing, ring-barking, pick-and-shovel work, harvesting ... anything and everything the bush had to offer'. Tom took 4-year-old Harry on the road, walking miles each day, jumping trains, surviving on ingenuity, begging for food and, on occasions, stealing. The necessities of life like food and shelter were no longer guaranteed. Out of the wretchedness of hard times, the pair developed a no-nonsense, self-reliant way of life.

> During the worst of it, my bed was the ground, my blankets the clothes I wore. My fire was the warmth of Dad's body; my only shelter his strong brown arms. He was the house that sheltered me and the church at which I worshipped.
>
> *(Reade, H. 1987, 34)*

The conditions father and son experienced together forged an extremely close bond between them. In a 1987 *Sydney Morning Herald* article, Reade recalled his father's 'cranky toughness' as he grew up in a world 'without caresses'. Yet he loved his father, and honoured his memory. He said that he 'could not understand the current fashion that insists that fathers regularly hug their children to demonstrate their affection' (Stephens, T. 1987, 45).

By late 1931, 28 percent of the work force in Australia was out of work. Internationally, industrial production in the capitalist world fell by 35 percent, the volume of world trade in manufactured goods fell by over 40 percent, and by 1932 over 30 million people were unemployed in the four major capitalist economies alone (Clark, D. 1981, 10–26). Workers became prisoners of poverty and the economic system, and stood in dole and ration queues.

Living from hand to mouth, Tom Reade found that handouts were few and far between as he looked for work in tough times. People who once thought they would rather die than beg would now sooner beg than ask for charity. Those who were out of work

FIGURE 1.1 Cover illustration for *An Elephant Charging My Chookhouse* drawn by Harry Reade. (Courtesy of Pat Evans.)

found themselves dependent on others. Workers without a job had to rely on their own cunning, self-reliance and ability to wrangle to survive. Knowing that 'the appeal of a four-year-old boy would elicit more response than that of a fifty-year-old man', Tom sent Harry to knock on the back doors of houses and ask, 'Please missus, Dad wants to know can you spare a bit of tea and sugar?' Mothers responded generously towards young Harry and he remembers the great pleasure he felt in their compassion:

> It is a joy I can now equate with opening packets under Christmas trees, finding Easter eggs, plunging your hand into a lucky dip, and scrabbling in the grass after a 'lolly shower' at a school picnic. I got *masses* of the stuff. Fruit and vegetables and cold meat, cupcakes with hundreds and thousands on top and a tin of sardines.
>
> (*Reade, H. 1987,* 42)

Associating begging with kindness, Harry warmed to his task. There was no stopping his innocent enthusiasm as he 'collected an embarrassment of food'. When it became apparent that this enterprise was spoiling Harry, his father called a halt to their food scavenging scheme. Overall, Reade's experience of the leanness of those years stoked his rage against society and his empathy with disadvantaged children. Years later, he learned to feel his father's shame and indignation at what a workless world had forced upon them both:

> In the burn of that shame and indignation, a Red was hardened. In every corner of this world where children are forced to beg and parents forced to let them, others are being forged of tougher metal. In those places where, as a better writer than I once put it, 'the grapes of wrath grow heavy for the vintage'. You don't like Reds ... you don't like revolutions? Then stop the hunger. The solution is as simple, and as uncomplicated, as that.
>
> (*Reade, H. 1987,* 43)

Community attitudes towards charity for the unemployed varied during the Great Depression. In his opus, *A History of Australia,* Manning Clark outlines one approach to dole relief for the unemployed during the 1930 New South Wales coal-mining dispute.

The All-Australian Trade Union Congress felt it was the primary duty of the Australian Government to provide unemployed workers with adequate food, clothing and shelter. Conservatives in power said that the dole 'corrupted morale, and withered individual initiative'. The church spoke of the duty of their members to distribute charity. Communists, however, held firm to the line that capitalism was the cause of worker's suffering and humiliation: it had 'degraded them into such pitiable creatures. They should fight the battle for socialism, not the verbal battle for the Australian back door'. In their view the dole and charity 'might blunt the revolutionary enthusiasm of the workers'. Beggars and tramps who knocked on suburban doors were 'scabs', corrupted human beings who indulged in 'a profusion of thanks and grovelling' (Clark, C. M. H. 1987, 338–339). This confronting attitude exacerbated Tom Reade's feeling of shame.

Memories of poverty and the generosity of farming communities left a lasting impression on Harry. Cuban colleague, ICAIC documentary director-cinematographer Harry Tanner, recalls Reade's hospitality and willingness to share when there was food rationing in Cuba during the 1960s. According to Tanner, Reade was a 'fantastic host' who was resourceful at gathering food. Being married to a Russian woman gave him access to a foreign technician's extra rations which he readily split with friends and visitors:

> His house was ever open for a good meal and maybe something to drink. He was a great improvisational cook … always going around on his motorcycle trying to see what he could scrounge up. He would get his own water chestnuts and bamboo shoots at places he knew on the banks of small rivers close to Havana. His fried rices and Xmas puddings were legendary.
>
> (*Tanner, H. 2006*, interview)

Tom and Harry Reade's itinerant life lasted 10 years. They travelled by train, foot, car, bicycle and horse and cart. Throughout their travels, his father carried one of his few possessions—a small parcel of books 'wrapped sailor-style, in oiled silk and canvas'.

> He parted with his overcoat to clothe me, his pride to feed me, but nothing would make him part with his books … Darwin's *Origin of Species*, Kropotkin's *Mutual Aid*, Marx and Engels's *Communist Manifesto* and Winwood Reade's *The Martydom of Man*.
>
> (*Reade, H. 1987, 56*)

Harry absorbed the currents of thought within these four tomes and they formed the cornerstone of his social and political credo. He points out that Kropotkin, a scientist who had led the anarchist movements in Russia and England during the late nineteenth and early twentieth centuries had argued in *Mutual Aid: A Factor of Evolution* that despite the Darwinian concept of the survival of the fittest, co-operation was the chief factor in the evolution of the species. The human race became the dominant species because it had the capacity to collaborate. From his understanding of the *Communist Manifesto*, Harry concluded that the logical epitome of collaboration was the commune in which all worked for the common good, and took from the common wealth according to individual needs. The logical extension of communal collaboration was global cooperation as envisaged in the *Martyrdom of Man*. In his unpublished manuscript, *A Funny Kind of Left-wing Animal*, Reade particularly acknowledges the influence of the *Martyrdom of Man* on his intellectual and political life. Listening to his father's regular readings of the book was intoxicating for him. The 'future' described by Winwood Reade became the shining star that Harry hitched himself to and referred to as 'the dream'. *A Funny Kind of Left-wing Animal* begins:

> It began as a dream and the dream became a book the old man held a little further from his eyes and a little closer to the light.… But the light was golden and the words

were golden and for the boy, elbows on knees and chin on hands, so was the moment. He watched and listened and lived in a softly ballooning world of wonder.... The words rolled on, the night passed and the years passed and the old man passed with them. But the dream continued and, one by one, things predicted in the old book came to pass as well.

(*Reade, H. 1998*)

On the road, Harry and his father slept wherever they could find shelter on the edges of settlements in southeast Australia—under bridges, in empty railway stations and in shantytowns of hessian-sack humpies. Many of the walls of these derelict shelters were covered with graffiti, which aroused and influenced his early interest in drawing:

Another camp—an abandoned house—I have always felt to be responsible for my early interest in drawing.... Every inch of the inside walls was covered with drawings, poems, quotations, names, decorations and commentary on the world. Drawings of pretty girls abounded—as pretty girls—and even the nudes were honest attempts at works of art. The heads of horses and old bearded men were popular subjects, as were complicated geometric patterns. The medium, naturally enough, was charcoal, although many of the drawings and most of the writing was in pencil, either lead or the then-common blue-one-end, red-the-other kind. The drawing that fascinated me was of a bicycle swaggie, complete in every detail—or so it seemed to my eyes then, though no doubt fondness of memory has since added to the artist's skill.

(*Reade, H. 1987,* 51–52)

Harry's lifestyle limited his formal schooling to just four years primary. The drifting life also deprived him of friendships with other children. During the long hours spent alone, while his father picked up work on farms, he nurtured his solitude by poring over comic strips in Sunday papers and wondering what the stories were about. He lists among his favourite titles, *Flash Gordon* and a weekly publication called *Wags*, which ran popular American and English strips like *Smokey Stover, Katzenjammer Kids, Terry and the Pirates, Casey Court* and Hogarth's *Tarzan*. Unlike syndicated American strips, English 'comic cuts' relied heavily on text below the panels to advance the narrative. From his appreciation of his father's ability to tell him what happened in the stories, Harry developed a keenness to read and, in time, a desire to write. This early literary enthusiasm—conjuring stories around comic strip layouts—enriched his formative years. Despite the absence of any formal training he taught himself how to construct drawings that carried messages. While recognising his son's developing skills, Tom Reade maintained a pragmatic view of vocational matters:

> My father applauded my increasing skill at writing and art but could see no practical use for it. He often spoke of my 'learning a trade' when I left school, spoke of engineering as 'a fine thing', and when my interest in art continued, suggested I might like to be a signwriter—'another good trade'. I was in my late twenties and had for some time more or less earned my living as a mediocre—albeit widely published—left-wing cartoonist before he changed his mind and expressed regret for not having encouraged me earlier.
>
> (*Reade, H. 1987,* 199)

Sustained hardship and unemployment endured by more than one-third of Australian wage earners fomented organised social protest. Not surprisingly, political and social activists found the 1930s a time full of purpose, and they demanded that the State find them work, not give them charity. Political movements emerged during this time advocating an alternative social system that guaranteed security, equality and freedom from the deprivations that a crisis-ridden capitalism had inflicted on Australia. The Communist Party of Australia (CPA) pointed to the long lines of unemployed as evidence that the old traditions and practices of the working class were about to be swept away (Farrell, F. 1981, 183). It was also able to proclaim that in the Union of Soviet Socialist Republics—one-sixth of the world—no man or woman willing to work went without the necessities of life.

Founded in 1920, within a decade or so the CPA had become a coherent ideological organisation. It had expanded membership from around 100 in the late 1920s to several thousand by the mid-1930s. Throughout the 1930s Tom Reade actively supported the CPA's platform. Its focus on organising the unemployed, women, anti-fascists and radical workers strengthened the Party's claim to be at the centre of anti-capitalist action (Symons, B., A. Wells and S. Mcintyre. 1994, viii). Against a panorama of political campaigns, Harry Reade's early ideological grounding was invested with an activist's temper. At the age of 7 he was helping his father paste posters in support of equal pay for women.

> Equal Pay for Equal Work! Support Women's Struggle! Support Egon Kisch! Demonstrate against von Luckner! Free Speech! No Scrap Iron for Japan! Public Meeting to Protest Unemployment! Public Meeting to Support Chinese People! There wouldn't have been a major left-wing campaign in the 1930s in which I did not participate in one way or another.
>
> (*Reade, H. 1987*, 107)

By 1940, the physical demands of bush labouring encouraged Tom Reade to search for easier work in the city. In Melbourne he found a job as a pastry-cook and, at the age of 13, Harry began work in a silversmith shop soldering the waterproof seams on teapot bodies. After a brief stint brazing copper at Avant Water Heaters, he secured a foundry job at Pressure Injected Castings where he die-cast domestic knives. The work lasted four years, and Harry recounted the harshness of the foundry, making do on low teen-age wages, the 'rough horseplay', the fights and brawls, foundry accidents, industrial strikes and mateship. He also recalled that, years later, the foundry boss Jimmy Feehan remembered him as 'a lazy bludging little bastard'. He retorted that if 'Feehan's own children grew up to enjoy the good life' it was 'at the expense of youths like him who did men's work for children's pocket money'. He added, 'I was no ragged-trousered philanthropist making a gift of my life to the boss'. Other memories of these years include reading in the State Library of Victoria, his sexual awakenings in Brunswick brothels, and the American troops who were stationed in Australia during World War II (WWII) (Reade, H. 1998).

At the age of 14, Reade joined the illegal Young Communist League (YCL). His father 'bumped up Harry's age' to meet the YCL membership lower age limit of 15 years and assured the organisation that he 'was big for it and old beyond'. The Australian Government imposed a ban on Communism in 1940–1941 when communists opposed and threatened to sabotage the WWII effort. When the ban was lifted in 1942 in recognition of the status of Soviet Russia as an ally against Nazi Germany, the YCL emerged as the legal Eureka Youth League (EYL), the youth front organ-isation of the CPA. Throwing its resources into the anti-fascist struggle, the CPA was able to demonstrate and extend its influ-ence not only in the industrial sphere, but also in the intellectual and cultural arenas of Australian life.

During the 1940s, the EYL 'was a vibrant entity where sport, music and protest came together under a flying red banner' (Fahey, W. 2004). It attracted a significant section of radical Australian youth impatient with the conservatism of post-war mainstream society. A documentary film, *Springwood Festival Camp*, produced in 1950 by the Realist Film Unit (Australia), depicts EYL camp activities in Springwood, NSW, and also at Camp Eureka, Yarra Junction, Melbourne. Several shots in the film capture young historian Wendy Lowenstein, as well as Harry Reade dressed in army uniform, sunglasses, and corncob pipe masquerading as General Douglas MacArthur, commander of Allied forces in the Southwest Pacific during WWII.

Harry was sympathetic with the EYL's focus on collective activity, but as a group member he was confronted by the tensions faced by an individualist in a communist milieu. EYL activities forced him to first recognise contradictions in his behaviour that were to challenge his ability to participate in cooperative achievements. In his autobiography, he states that his 'bloodlines were one hundred percent proletarian … and [he] was the son of a long time communist—the ideal stuff which a "cadre" do make'. He also acknowledges that his inability to toe the EYL party line on social idealism caused him to be 'a fly in the ointment'. 'I didn't take long to disillusion them … they reached the conclusion that I would never be a leader, and furthermore, would prove difficult to lead' (Reade, H. 1998). Artist, Clem Millward, who worked with Harry Reade on the Sydney waterfront during the 1950s, corroborates this view and remembers the crusty Reade as:

> … a difficult person to work with because he was not able to follow. He had to be in charge of things. Harry was abrasive with anyone who treated him without respect, or who expressed anti-humanist or anti-worker sentiments.
> (*Millward, C. 2005,* interview)

Reade left a common impression of his personality and behaviour with those who knew him. Cuban colleague Harry Tanner described him as 'a curmudgeon with a personal viewpoint on everything' (Tanner, H. 2006, interview). Founding member of the Waterside Workers' Federation Film Unit, Norma Disher recalled that:

> He pushed one's patience quite a long way. It was almost as though he was pushing you in some way to reject him…. I think Harry was an incredibly talented human being who

made life extremely difficult for himself.... There was an element in him which kind of blew-up or undermined a lot of the things he was brilliant at. His relationships, I think, would have been of great torment to him.

(*Disher, N. 2005*, interview).

Reade's friend, journalist and former production editor of *The Sunday Australian*, David Evans, added:

[He] looked like a wharfie. He was big—not heavily built but solidly built—and he looked like a 'tough'; you know, you'd look at him in a pub and say, 'Jesus, I wouldn't like to meet him in a dark alley'. But, in fact, he was exactly the opposite. I mean, he was an incredibly sensitive person and very, very generous to anybody. He was fairly quick to take offence if you said something he didn't agree with—not in an aggressive sense but it sort of upset him if you didn't agree with him or you didn't think the same way that he did.

(*Evans, D. 2005*, interview)

In spite of his 'difficult' social behaviour and anarchist streak, at the age of 17, Harry became a member of the CPA.

During his twenties, he drifted through a variety of jobs. He made auto parts for a Melbourne company called Disco. He was a lithographic artist for Victory Publicity, a street photographer, fisherman, pick and shovel worker, rabbit shooter, able-bodied seaman and steel mill worker.

Tensions between three socio-political forces helped shape the character of Australian society in the post-WWII years. Firstly, the fear that peace may not last was marked by the anxieties of the Cold War. Secondly, with the outbreak of war in Korea in 1952, the nation experienced strong economic growth and a developing consumer culture. The vast majority of the population benefited from improved living standards and the unemployment rate never went higher than 3 percent. Thirdly, economic prosperity nurtured individual investment in domesticity promising security, marital commitment and private happiness (Murphy, J. 2000, 81). However, despite increasing prosperity, for many working class people, some of the immediate difficulties encountered during the era of 'consensus and conformity' were concerns for a shortage of basic foods and essentials, health services, critical housing shortages, and limited opportunities (Waterhouse, R. 1995, 199). In response to these underlying social contradictions, dissenting, so-called 'anti-Australian' voices challenged the prosperity of the nation.

The most militant and organised of these voices was the CPA. During WWII, public acceptance of a more independent foreign policy, wartime controls and economic planning implemented by the Australian Government, provided the CPA with the opportunity to develop 'a perspective that was both internationalist and able to capture the spirit of the Australian radical nationalist tradition. Writers, painters, historians and a politicised public made a deep impact on Australia's wartime and post-war cultural developments' (Symons, B., A. Wells and S. Mcintyre. 1994, viii). By war's end, the CPA had a membership of 20,000 that was linked to the program of post-war reconstruction through the union movement. This put the Party into a position of significant influence. The CPA's aim of developing the labour movement and uniting workers naturally gravitated towards trade unions. Historian Geoffrey Bolton points out, however, that the extent of Communist influence in the Australian trade unions was hard to gauge 'because conservatives unfriendly to the Labor movement tended to label any militant left-winger as an out-and-out communist. Industrially they were enough of a nuisance to give credence to the anti-communists, particularly since strikes frequently happened in the sectors of industry that hit the public' (Bolton, G. C. 1974, 494).

During the immediate post-war period, an important aspect of national progress that threatened the CPA's influence was an increasing emphasis on the role of the individual—politically, economically and socially—and a decreasing emphasis on the collective body or the group action. In the workplace, personal achievement incentives and individual accountability were embraced ahead of co-operative techniques (Milner, L. 2003, 11). Communist candidates never gained more than 1.5 percent of the total vote cast at federal elections in the 1940s.

The CPA's influence over unions was challenged during this period by industrial groups within the Australian Labor Party (ALP). The ALP had interpreted the CPA's industrial influence as a bid for political capital. A struggle ensued and came to a head in 1949, with the outcome of the prolonged Coal Strike. Labor Prime Minister Ben Chifley saw the event as a communist challenge to the Federal Labor Government's power in the labour movement, and used the army to break the strike. Failure of the strike signalled a major defeat for the labour movement at large, particularly the CPA, which lost considerable influence and political strength in the trade union movement. The CPA's policy of industrial aggression was also discredited in the eyes of most Australian workers 'largely because the "ordinary public", being so seriously affected, resented these strikes and the Communist Party's part in them' (Fitzgerald, R. 1984, 134).

In the 1949 federal election, Robert Menzies and his Liberal-Country Party coalition defeated the Chifley Government and ushered in 23 years of unbroken conservative rule. In 1951, Menzies sought to increase his government's power by attempting to ban the Communist Party, but a referendum held to this end was defeated. Despite this, by the end of the 1950s the CPA membership had declined to less than 6000. In the industrial sphere, it had been forced back to its traditional base among a heavy industrial and largely masculine workforce. It lost many of its non-working-class members, and with their departure, its intellectual and cultural activities lost much of their vitality (Symons, B., A. Wells and S. Mcintyre. 1994, viii).

From 1949 and throughout the 1950s, a conservative Australian Government challenged communist influence through the

Australian Security Intelligence Organisation's (ASIO) surveillance of CPA members and suspected sympathisers. The Federal Government's great fear was that in wartime the CPA might have instigated strikes in national industries or in some way sabotaged them to serve the interests of the United Soviet Socialist Republic (USSR). During the 1949 Coal Strike, Harry Reade was employed at the Broken Hill Pty Company's (BHP) steel works in Newcastle. As a known communist, his activities were monitored by ASIO. Their files note that at public meetings, during the Coal Strike, Harry was regarded as a communist 'strong arm' man. Further, he was 'strongly suspected of being responsible for a fire, which destroyed a section of the BHP works known as the subliming plant' (ASIO. Henry Garbutt Reade. File 17).

While the incident bears the hallmarks of the Wobblies' concept of 'direct action' at the workplace, Reade asserts in his autobiography that he was just 'pushing a skip when it happened'. Perhaps he was responsible, but it was not in his interests to start it. This was because shortly before the fire, he had 'sounded out' the other workers about electing a shop steward for his section. They indicated that they were reluctant to support 'commos' but said they would vote for him if such a meeting were held. It never was, because the subliming plant fire intervened (Reade, H. 1998). Because of his communist affiliation, Harry Reade was of particular interest to police when workers were questioned about the blaze. In a 1996 television documentary, he contemptuously dismissed ASIO's report by declaring that the organisation had 'diddled the Australian public'. Of the 'strong-arm man' claims, he said he 'couldn't fight his way out of a paper bag' and that the 'bloody fire nearly burned me' (Gunzburg, D. 1996).

Following the BHP steel works fire incident, Harry was blacklisted and found it hard to earn a living in Newcastle. He headed south and maintained his peripatetic lifestyle while working for short periods in a variety of jobs. His working class background and self-education had shaped him as a confident and resourceful person who could go it alone. He was used to surviving on little in the way of resources. In 1954, he married Joy 'Nicki' Dent in Sydney. Little is known of this short-lived relationship and it receives scant mention in his autobiography. Reade's colleagues have recalled the marriage but could not offer any reasons for its demise.

In a *Sydney Morning Herald* interview, in 1987, Harry reflected on the years spent on the road with his Wobbly father and the impact they had on the formation of his intellectual and political life:

> My father's life had made him a Red, and our lives together combined with the exploitation of a child labourer to make *me* a Red, just as Jack London and Victor Gaunt, Master Spy, combined to make me a hopeless romantic…. Alan Francis, a schoolteacher [at Tallangatta Primary School], and Charles Dickens and a thousand others made me an artist, and all combined to make a rainbow chaser.
>
> (*Stephens, T. 1987,* 45)

Reade's personality carried the imprint of his years on the road with his father and his efforts to earn a living. Always vehemently anti-capitalist, he was attracted to work in sectors of industry represented by militant trade unions: those led by officials who had won approval from their members as effective fighters for their grievances. The Sydney waterfront would soon provide an environment within which he could integrate his ideological beliefs with creative expression.

NOTE

1. Thomas Paine (1737–1809) was born in Norfolk, England. In the *Rights of Man*, Paine attacked hereditary government and argued for equal political rights. He suggested that all men over 21 in Britain should be given the vote and this would result in a House of Commons willing to pass laws favourable to the majority. The book also recommended progressive taxation, family allowances, old age pensions, maternity grants and the abolition of the House of Lords. Paine is acknowledged as one of the Founding Fathers of the United States of America.

CHAPTER 2

On the Waterfront

HARRY READE'S CREATIVE INFLUENCES AND DEVELOPMENT (1954–1956)

In 1954, Harry Reade became a wharfie on the Sydney waterfront where the cultural activity of the workforce was sustained through the support of its militant trade union, the Waterside Workers' Federation (WWF). He became part of a collective of artist-workers whose collaboration inspired links between cultural activity and the industrial and political struggles of the WWF. This experience set Reade on a path towards a career in animation.

When Harry began work as a wharf labourer, the job of loading and unloading cargo ships on the Sydney waterfront was undertaken on a series of wharves, which extended from Circular Quay to Walsh Bay, Miller's Point and Darling Harbour. Men who walked the length of the docks in search of employment knew the stretch as 'The Hungry Mile'. Despite the arduous nature of work and the unreliability of periodic employment, Harry was attracted to it because the casual employment conditions were offset by the potential to do long shifts which meant that it was possible to earn in two or three days what might otherwise take a week. Historian Margo Beasley describes the bonds that were forged between

wharf labourers in *Wharfies: a History of the Waterside Workers'*
Federation of Australia:

> There were diverse cargoes and great variety in wharf
> labouring, it was done outdoors which was often pre-
> ferred to inside work, and there was pleasure in working
> close to the sea and around ships from foreign places.
> Perhaps more importantly, great mateship and camara-
> derie developed in the close dependence fostered by bru-
> tal working conditions, and in the long waiting periods
> between jobs. Additionally, beyond homes and pubs, the
> only significant unifying structure that bound the com-
> munity together (the men more especially) was the union.
> The staunch fraternity and militancy which developed
> in these circumstances became the hallmarks of wharf
> labouring unionism in twentieth century Australia.
>
> (*Beasley, M. 1996*, 20)

Prior to the federation of Australian colonies in 1901, private shipping companies serviced trade to and from the country's ports
and owned most Australian wharves. Considerable growth in
the shipping industry during the late nineteenth century, however, exposed the inadequacies of many of these facilities. In New
South Wales, the Harbour Act of 1900 gave the State Government
control of the Port of Sydney, but after Federation both levels of
government began to contribute to the infrastructure on which
shipping relied. Despite improvements, systems of employing
labour and issues of health and safety made wharf labouring work
difficult, unpleasant, dangerous and irregular.

In 1904, the Federal Government established a Commonwealth
Arbitration Court which led many unions to seek amalgama-
tion or federation with organisations in other states in order to
capitalise on the expected benefits and economies of scale that
national arbitration might bring. Formed in 1902, the WWF
became a national trade union under the leadership of future

Prime Minister, William 'Billy' Morris Hughes—then a New South Wales politician whose seat of Lang took in Sydney's wharf labouring communities. Hughes' early political ambitions were nurtured by energetic involvement in industrial organisations and as secretary of the Sydney Wharf Labourers' Union—a precursor to the WWF—he negotiated an agreement with employers for general uniformity of wages and conditions among shipping companies (Beasley, M. 1996, 17–20).

The WWF Sydney Branch occupied a small building at 60 Sussex Street, which was located next to the wharves. The premises provided little in the way of amenities other than a shelter for workers waiting for the daily 'pick-up' by stevedoring company foremen. The 'pick-up' or 'bull' system used by employers to engage casual labour pitted wharf labourers against each other. The strongest men, or 'bulls', were favoured for work. This method of engaging labour favoured compliant and docile workers and facilitated discrimination against militant or troublesome men who might agitate for improved conditions. It was not uncommon for such wharf labourers to be left without work or income for weeks on end—a system fraught with bribery and corruption (Beasley, M. 1996, 19–20).

Leading the WWF through its most militant and influential years was the charismatic General Secretary, Jim Healy, who assumed the position in 1937. As a member of the CPA, Healy followed the Party's position on many issues. He was also part of 'an outstanding generation of activists who had experienced the hardship and hunger of the depression and brought strategic skill to the struggle against capitalism'. Under Healy's leadership, the forthright industrial objectives of the WWF were equalisation of work, shorter hours, better pay and safer working conditions.

In 1943, the 'bull' system of daily labour recruitment was replaced by the Gang System under which men became members of a regular gang effectively of their own choosing and foremen lost the right to pick and choose who worked where. By 1946, Saturday pick-ups were abolished and members were paid attendance money. The gang system underpinned the camaraderie that developed among WWF members and fostered a core feature of WWF strength that relied on deep and personal relationships. The system also accommodated the creation of common interest groups, which in turn forged strong bonds between members:

> The element of choice involved in gang selection allowed groups of men to form around political allegiances (militant, moderate and others) or around more personal relationships (fathers, sons, brothers and friends). Many gangs were like extended families in which the members were aware of, and shared in, important events in each other's lives; births, deaths, illnesses and hard times.
>
> *(Beasley, M. 1996,* 102–118)

For many artists and intellectuals, casual employment on the wharves gave them flexibility and extra time to devote to interests outside of work. Harry Reade became a member of Gang 364, which was comprised of people interested in a variety of creative disciplines. Fellow gang member, Clem Millward gives a sense of the close connection members enjoyed in work and recreation:

> They used to call us 'The Brains Trust'. We used to play chess in the rain periods and smokos and so on. We had a very talented composer, Arnold Butcher… and people who were trying to write and act and all this sort of thing, all in the same gang.
>
> *(Millward, C. 2005,* interview)

In 1959, newspaper columnist, editor of *Quadrant* magazine and observer of trade union activity, P. P. (Paddy) McGuiness shared a flat in Balmain with Harry Reade. McGuiness believed that Harry was attracted to work on the wharves because the WWF was committed to militant industrial action:

Being a wharfie was a fashionable thing to do if you were a communist or extreme Left. It had a romantic image—all strikes and the history. Of course it was dominated at that stage by the Communist Party.

(McGuinness, P. 2005, interview)

As Australia entered the first years of the post-War period, the WWF achieved further advances. New overtime limits were set, a uniform method of sling-loading cargo was developed, better annual leave was gained and industrial clothing and safety gear was introduced. Ambulance posts were also established on the wharves. These successes further boosted the spirit of solidarity between the union and its members as 'unionists took on a greater sense of pride in their identity as wharfies, as workers and unionists'. By 1957, at the height of its popularity, the union could boast a national membership of 27,000 (Milner, L. 2003, 17–18). The gains made by the WWF were seen at the time as establishing the union's independence, and artistic and cultural activities soon gained prominence as an expression of that independence (Reeves, A. 1992, 6).

CULTURAL CONTEXT OF THE SYDNEY WATERFRONT

The Communist Party's official directive on cultural production was based on Lenin's 1917 edict, 'art is a weapon', which exhorted artists to use creativity as a political tool in defence of worker's rights (Eisenstein, S. 1930). The style through which this ideology was expressed was *socialist realism*. In *Of Storm and Struggle: Pages from Labour History*, Edgar Ross stated this was the Party line adopted by the CPA in the mid-1940s: 'The arts constitute one of the most important spheres of activity in the deep-going ideological struggle between decadent capitalism and the forces making for human liberation' (Ross, E. 1982, 128).

Under Healy's leadership and influence of the CPA, the WWF supported an ideal that encouraged the cultural and artistic self-development of its members. The Federation's position engendered the formation of waterside workers' creative groups and an upsurge in cultural activity which served a number of purposes:

> In addition to representing a principal source of collective experience and memory, it also provided a focus for self-identification and served to extend union-related activities beyond regulated hours of work into the realm of recreation and relaxation. Cultural activities also provided an increasingly popular medium for giving expression to a range of political objectives and social aspirations, with an effectiveness that no flood of pamphlets could hope to emulate.
>
> (*Reeves, A. 1992*, 12)

Clem Millward had worked in commercial art studios in Sydney before studying drawing and painting in Bucharest from 1951 to 1955. He recalled the attraction of casual wharf labour and the convenient location of the WWF's Sydney Branch building which was next to the docks:

> It was a job that suited me … at that stage, you had to go into the 'pick-up' centre in the morning…and stand there while all the numbers were called out. If you were allocated a job you 'hot-footed' it around to that particular wharf. If you didn't get a job, then you were in the middle of the city with a day off. So I began drawing and painting upstairs in the union rooms.
>
> (*Millward, C. 2005*, interview)

In 1950 with fund's derived from record membership, the union upgraded the Sussex Street amenities. The aim was to provide facilities for WWF members to participate in collective recreation. Extensive renovations undertaken during 1951–1952 enabled the Branch to offer members a canteen, art studio, a new hall, facilities for film production and musical performances as well as a library and reading room.

In the early 1950s, with the majority of its members living in close proximity to the docks, the Sydney waterfront represented 'a geographically concentrated force of power'. It was also a close community with strong loyalties and a sense of solidarity. Workers knew each other's fathers, sons, brothers, in-laws and neighbours. Unionists and their families did not have far to travel to participate in after-work events at the Branch hall, which became the community's cultural centre. Inside its walls, the internal life of the waterside community was sustained by recreational activities, political activism, education, sport and entertainment (Reeves, A. 1992, 12). During lunchtime and after work, wharfies and their families filled the hall to participate in concerts, recitals, dance performances and lectures. Fellow 'Brains Trust' member Jock Levy recalls his contribution to the Sydney Branch's cultural activities:

> Amongst those people who went into the Federation at that particular time were a number of artists...who had been in theatre, like myself. The union premises had a pretty shallow sort of stage and I asked Tommy Nelson, who was secretary of the Sydney Branch of the WWF if I could put a play on. He put it to the committee and they said, "Yes, go ahead." That was the first play [*The Travellers* by Ewan McColl] put on by the WWF, mainly by members of the 'old' New Theatre.
>
> (*Levy, J. 2005,* interview)

THE STUDIO OF REALIST ART AND THE WHARFIES ART GROUP

One group of professional artists which applied the WWF's approach to cultural and artistic self-development was the Studio of Realist Art (SORA). SORA had been officially formed by a group of contemporary artists and their supporters on 2 March 1945. Operating in a three-roomed basement backing onto the waterfront in Sussex Street, Sydney, the studio was established to generate a cultural climate sympathetic to radical action in society through creative activity. SORA declared its purpose in the first edition of its newsletter, *Bulletin*:

> It is natural that such a group as ours should come into existence, in opposition to the large amount of other-worldly, art-for-art's sake that fills the walls of so many exhibitions—work that is an expression of decadence and puerility, that is impossible to relate to the mass of Australian people. People are showing in no uncertain fashion their dislike of the 'nostalgic' idea, the classical subject of the ivory tower complete with artists who 'look down on the world', by their support for such organisations as the Encouragement of Art Movement...and now the Studio of Realist Art. Art is no longer the prerogative of a few but is rapidly becoming the concern of many.
>
> (*SORA Bulletin*. 1945, (1))

Foundation members of SORA included art historian, Bernard Smith, and artists Roy Dalgarno, Rod Shaw, John Oldham, Hal Missingham and James Cant. Cant had participated in several anti-fascist exhibitions through the Artists' International Association. His conception of a radical culture embodied aesthetic and political dimensions and set the tone for SORA. The group attempted to forge direct links with the trade union movement through lectures, art classes, social events and plans for communal art projects. Although all of the SORA founding members, except Missingham, were members of the Communist Party, the group's activities were 'intended to parallel Party political activity rather than serve it slavishly'. By relating art to the needs of ordinary men and women, SORA leaders urged workers to become artists (Haese, R. 1982, 171–175).

In *Rebels and Precurors*, Richard Haese provides a framing discourse for the development of Australian art during the years spanning the Great Depression and the Cold War. He stresses that the 1930s and 1940s were marked by an intense political climate of ideological crusades and cynical opportunism, conflicting claims between nationalism and internationalism and the impact of economic depression and total war on cultural forms. Haese also argues that Australian radical art at this time reflected a search for new social and intellectual roles for art and the artist:

> What characterised that art above all else was a deep and pervasive concern for realism, the reality of human social and psychological experience at a time of unremitting crisis and intellectual struggle.
>
> (*Haese, R. 1982*, vii–ix)

During the early 1950s, SORA supported and encouraged interested WWF members to establish the Wharfies Art Group. Clem Millward recalls the group's beginnings:

> The Group's formation was intended to get wharfies interested, working and painting really. There were a number of them who…worked on May Day banners and that sort of thing.
>
> (*Millward, C. 2005*, interview)

Stimulated by the creative alliance between SORA and the WWF, Reade became a member of the Wharfies' Art Group. Prior to becoming a wharfie, his interest in art practice had been steadily increasing. In *A Funny Kind of Left-wing Animal*, he states that he was beginning to develop skills for which he had no outlet, but 'art is like the man who will not let me be'. Taking part-time jobs in Melbourne, he studied painting under Murray Griffin at the National Art Gallery. Griffin had been appointed an official war artist in 1941. With the fall of Singapore, he was taken prisoner of war by the Japanese in February 1942. In the Changi prisoner-of-war camp, he produced paintings and drawings that showed the life and activities of the prisoners. Under Griffin's tuition Reade came to consider that in his own art, 'the raw talent was there'. Nevertheless, he expressed anxiety about art's purpose:

> What was I to do with the results? My whole life my political orientation filled me with a desire, a need to paint my people and paint for them, but the only people who could afford to buy my paintings were those whose pockets could pay, but whose hearts I couldn't hope to touch, or as Party jargon put it, 'move to action'.
>
> (*Reade, H. 1998*)

Stating that he came to 'the conclusion that no painting ever moved anyone to action', Reade cites Pablo Picasso's anti-fascist painting *Guernica*, claiming that his portrayal of civilian suffering during the Spanish Civil War was 'incomprehensible to my working class eyes'. The painting was suffering made 'safe and decorative ... suffering one could hang on one's dining room wall and discuss without feeling queasy over dessert' (Reade, H. 1998). Among his teachers at the time Reade lists the noted social realist artist, Noel Counihan, whose cartoons he 'greatly admired'. With such antipathy to the decorative bourgeois practice of 'art-for-art's sake', Reade clearly empathised with SORA's manifesto. Yet, he also had difficulty toeing the line with the strictly sanctioned communist art of social realism.

His views on art found him coming into conflict with the official Communist Party line, specifically, its definition of 'socialist' as opposed to 'social' realism. The Party's edict stressed that *social* realism was merely a mirror, while *socialist* realism 'pointed the way forward'. Reade illustrates his dilemma when attempting to integrate social consciousness with painting:

> I did the best I could but when I painted one of my people— an old pensioner pushing her pram-load of possessions

down a North Melbourne street—I couldn't for the life of
me, see a way to give it a 'positive' message. Stick a *Guardian*
seller on the next corner with her walking towards him?
Put a chalked slogan on the wall—*Join ... You have nothing
to lose but your chains!*? I settled for making a sarcastic reference to a recent speech by Prime Minister Chifley. Called
it *Golden Age* and let things go at that.

(*Reade, H. 1998*)

In *Place, Taste and Tradition*, Bernard Smith describes 'social
realist' artists as those concerned with 'the human drama of
their time'. He contends that their work 'reveal[s] social truths'
and 'affirm[s] the social value of art...by reacting directly to
the world of experience' (Smith, B. 1945, 239–242). *Socialist*
realism, on the other hand, was understood as propagandistic
illustrations of Communist Party dogma (Burn, I., et al. 1987,
69). Millward offered his understanding of social realism and
commented on the work of prominent Australian social realist
artists:

It was a socially conscious art. Noel Counihan is the
classic social realist. Albert Tucker, in his way, was a
social realist but also a symbolist in his treatment of
social problems. Jim Wigley was another social realist
who painted the conditions of aborigines throughout
the late '40's and '50's. Ray Dalgano, who did series of
drawings of miners, seamen and other workers, was
also a significant representative of the SORA group....
I did a number of lino-cuts of old wharf labourer's
faces.... I had a title at the beginning of the set: *These
are the faces of men who survived the horrors of the
First World War but could not speak about them, and
who endured the humiliations of the Depression years
and could never forget them.*

(*Millward, C. 2005*, interview)

The proximity of SORA's basement premises to the WWF build-ing in Sussex Street facilitated contacts between 'left-leaning and artistically inclined wharfies' and the SORA artists for whom the worker's viewpoint was central to the expression of their move-ment. SORA supported and encouraged art classes with WWF members interested in developing drawing and painting skills as well as exploring their own artistic inclinations. Reade and other wharfie artists generally produced placards, billboards and ban-ners displayed in May Day parades during the 1940s and 1950s, but their association with SORA artists generated a rich cross-fertilisation of information, ideas and energies. They participated in 'a network of political alliances, personal friendships, shared studios, theories of art and social philosophies that collectively linked their work and lives' (Reeves, A. 1992, 26–27). The close connection between the two groups was a demonstration of the way in which art, unionism and politics could be creatively inte-grated. This successful alliance therefore justified Healy's efforts to allocate WWF funds to support the cultural and artistic self-development of its members.

THE SYDNEY WHARFIES' MURAL

Reade's individual paintings do not appear to have survived; how-ever, he made a significant contribution to the Sydney Wharfies' Mural. This work is an enduring expression of the cultural fer-ment and collaboration between trade union activists and wharfie artists and extends 7.5 metres and stands 2.5 metres tall.

Between 1953 and 1965, the mural was painted on a wall of the Sydney Waterside Workers' Hall canteen. SORA artist Roderick Shaw inspired and led the project that was conceived as a co-operative work of art for the Wharfie's Art Group. The mural illustrates key aspects of Australia's economic and social life and parallel histories of the Australian labour movement, trade unions and the WWF over a period of almost a century.

Andrew Reeves explained the cultural significance of this historical document:

> The mural is a roll call of the union's battle honours, representing the traditions on which the union was built, the communities which have sustained it, and the collective political and industrial experiences that have shaped its character and vision.
>
> *(Reeves, A. 1991–1992, 202–203)*

The work underwent three principal periods of development with many wharfie artists contributing to the finished piece. Clem Millward and Harry Reade were associated with the 'middle years' of its creation. Millward, who painted during his free time in the upstairs rooms of the Union's building, remembers the mural's progress:

> [Rod Shaw] stopped working on it because they were going to pull the rooms down and it seemed like a fruitless thing to continue. I used to sit there in front of this thing having my lunch and I decided that I would like to put some colour onto it. So I spoke to Rod and he said 'Yes, go ahead, but they're going to pull the whole thing down'. Anyway I started on it and was working my way across it when Harry decided that he was going to have a go too. We both brought colour into most of this monochromatic drawing.
>
> *(Millward, C. 2005, interview)*

By the late 1960s, new methods of handling cargoes affected the historic finger wharves on the Sydney waterfront. They were replaced with larger wharves to accommodate new ships and loading technology, especially containerisation. This led to associated changes in work arrangements and a corresponding shift in the local community to outer Sydney suburbs. It also led to a decline in use of the union's Sussex Street building which was sold in 1991. The mural was transferred from the walls of the canteen to new union offices at 61–63 Sussex Street and finally to the National Maritime Museum at Darling Harbour.

READE THE CARTOONIST

During a period of escalating cultural activity on the waterfront, Reade maintained his childhood enthusiasm for drawing and steadily developed into an accomplished cartoonist. Typically his cartoons projected a combination of his ideologies and his working class sense of humour. Commenting on the influences on his work in *A Funny Kind of Left-wing Animal*, Reade describes the influences on the content of his cartoons:

> I just kept drawing things because I couldn't help it. They had little in common with what is accepted as political cartooning today...funny little characters doing funny little things. I was under the influence of Daumier and Forian...of Claude Marquet, Will Dyson, America's Bob Minor and Bill Gropper. Simple stuff, drawn dramatically. A horse with a union label throwing the boss out of the saddle ... a fat capitalist labelled *Dailey Press* waving a scarecrow labelled *That Old Red Bogey* ... stuff like that.

In 1996, Harry Reade was the subject of *Twilight Rebel*, a documentary made by the Australian Broadcasting Commission for its *Australian Story* series. In it, he explained his attitude towards art and political cartooning. He echoed Lenin's 'art is a weapon' edict and was unambiguous in his view that the artist was capable of mobilising an audience into action:

> I always wanted to be a cartoonist. At the same time I wanted to do something. I thought, well.... Art never moved anybody. But you could fire cartoons like bullets

in the front line. I used to get a kick out of, you know, up
in the coal mines they'd get one of my cartoons and cut it
out and stick it up. I used to like that in Cuba too. I'd go
around and see my cartoons stuck on doors, all over the
island.

(Twilight Rebel, 1996)

The vitality of an active labour sector in Australia during the
1950s led to an increase in the publication of industrial and political newspapers, journals and magazines. These were circulated
and supported by large numbers of union members. In *Industrial
Labour and Politics,* Ian Turner argued that these sources assisted
the conversion of unionists into 'social levers in their own right'
(Turner, I. 1965, xvii). Working as a wharfie, Reade typified
Turner's 'social lever' concept by expressing his views through
cartoons and illustrations published in the CPA's national newspaper, *Tribune.* With these he asserted counter-commentaries to
the prevailing national political mood.

By 1958, Reade's cartoons began appearing under the panel
heading, *As Reade Sees It.* Paddy McGuiness claimed that the
issues motivating Reade's material were: 'whatever the fashionable
causes were in the Communist Party at the time and, of course,
being a cartoonist he was often sending up Menzies and the government of the day' (McGuinness, P. 2005, interview) (Figure 2.1).

Harry's press cartoons brought him to the attention of ASIO as
in 1949 when he wrote articles and drew cartoons for the Eureka
Youth League's *Youth Voice.* ASIO files contain copies of his illustrations and cartoon work. The selection provides an insight into
the Government's conservatism and Cold War vigilance. The files
note that Reade also contributed to the EYL's national newspaper
Challenge and the CPA's weekly *Tribune* (ASIO. Henry Garbutt
Reade. File 12).

By the late 1950s, the graphic style of Reade's political cartoons
had evolved from tight hard-edged brush and nib outlines to confident, loose scratchy nib-lines. The early sinuous style of figures

As Reade sees it...

"FOSTER world peace . . . foster trade with China. What a lot of rot. My policy is Foster Dulles . . ."

FIGURE 2.1 Cartoon of Prime Minister Robert Menzies drawn by Harry Reade. (Published in *Tribune*, 24 September 1958. Courtesy of Harry Reade's estate. Permission granted by executor of Reade's estate, Pat Evans.)

was replaced by a more carefree and unpolished delineation of forms. His panel compositions show figures uncluttered by excessive shading or background detail, and many are accompanied by a didactic text. His illustrations for articles were rendered in black and white, using scraper-board, charcoal and pen and ink. They all communicate anti-capitalist, anti-imperialist and labour struggle themes, and reflect social realist values that honour Australian working class icons and the world of labour. Many of his illustrations are bold chiaroscuro exercises, which exude grandeur and emotional power. Of his political cartoons Reade said, 'If any of them helped to save a miner's job, or a steelworker's eyes and hands, or helped to move people to reject McCarthyism and atomic war, I'm well satisfied' (Reade, H. 1998) (Figure 2.2).

In 1957, Harry composed a poem to honour the centenary of the birth of Henry Lawson, Australia's most famous rhyming

FIGURE 2.2   Wharfies labouring in a ship's hold drawn by Harry Reade. (Published in *Tribune*, 22 August 1956. Courtesy of Harry Reade's estate. Permission granted by the executor of Reade's estate, Pat Evans.)

commentator on social and political issues and occasional 'banger of the revolutionary drum'. The poem was constructed in a rhyme-scheme sympathetic with that used in many of Lawson's verses, and it was accompanied by a dramatic black and white, charcoal and ink portrait. When it was published in *Tribune,* 'Noel Counihan wrote to praise the drawing of Henry, but said I'd made the face too sensitive. It'll be a cold day in hell before I'll say anything against Noel living or dead … but he was wrong' (Reade, H. 1998).

In 1953, Reade began his own *Challenge* column called *Reade between the Lines* which he used to express his views and hone his writing skills. His working class sarcasm is evident in his response to a newspaper advertisement for a fur coat of 'blended wild mink'. He wrote, 'Stein and I are getting Aunt Myrtle a fur coat, as soon as we get his rabbit trap out of hock, that is' (Reade, H. 1953).

He was soon producing lengthier works of prose. A *Challenge* article records him as having been placed second in its 1953 short story competition, with a piece called *The Needle's Eye.* The entries were judged by Australian author Frank Hardy who praised Reade's work for 'the real excellence of the prose' and stated that he 'would have placed it first if its message had been explicit' (ASIO. Henry Garbutt Reade. File 13).

WATERSIDE WORKERS' FEDERATION FILM UNIT

In 1956, a significant event that gave impetus to Reade's creative progress occurred when he became involved in an initiative of the small radical Waterside Workers' Federation Film Unit (WWFFU)—the only trade union film unit in Australia. It was formed in 1953 by Norma Disher, Keith Gow and Jock Levy who were members of the left-wing New Theatre group.[1] All three were also members of the CPA, and Levy and Gow worked together on the waterfront in Gang 364—the same Gang as Harry Reade—the Brains Trust. Lisa Milner describes the three

members of the WWFFU as 'left cultural activists' who shared
a number of traits:

> They had strongly-held opinions on the nature of social
> justice, and faith in the utility of collective action. They
> relied on informal networks of communication and asso-
> ciation, and they often aimed to provide not just artistic
> but political training.
>
> (*Milner, L. 2003,* 19)

Norma Disher recalled the circumstances surrounding the establishment of the film unit:

> The unit was formed as a consequence of the production
> of a play, called *The Travellers* [by Ewan McColl]. The
> three of us were involved in producing, directing and pre-
> senting in the Union rooms. Keith and Jock made a trailer
> to screen to the wharfies. It was shown to the members
> so that they'd know there were performances each week
> for a number of weeks. One of the members who saw the
> trailer reported to the secretary, Tom Nelson, that two
> wharfies had made a short film and as a consequence they
> were asked if they could make a documentary film [sup-
> porting a campaign seeking pensions for veteran water-
> side workers] for the Union.
>
> (*Disher, N. 2005,* interview)

The WWFFU operated in Sydney from 1953 to 1958 and made
14 films. The films were consistent in their commitment to social
and industrial issues presented from the worker's point of view.
They presented a range of subjects concerned with workers' rights,
conditions, health, industrial disputes, campaigns for pensions
and the post-War housing shortage. In the period leading to the
unit's establishment, the labour movement's successes in gaining
better conditions of employment for its members had proved its

strength. The relatively expansive industrial climate allowed for a space where non-essential activities could be funded. Along with active union publishing in newspapers, journals and magazines, the film unit sought to 'consolidate the understanding of the use of film as a powerful propaganda weapon in their struggles for justice and social progress' (*Maritime Worker.* 1956, 2). In 1954, Sydney Branch Secretary, Tom Nelson, outlined the desired aims of the WWFFU:

> To bring, in a dramatic and educational form, the policy of the Federation to its members.
>
> To inform other trade unionists of the current struggles of the Waterside Workers and to enlist their support.
>
> To help create good relations with all sections of the community and to assist to make and develop independent working class films with other trade unions and working class organisations.

Among the Unit's titles were *Pensions for Veterans* (1953), *The Hungry Mile* (1955), *November Victory* (1955) and WWF Newsreel No.1 (1956). The latter recorded a strike in support of the Margins Dispute (the increase in margin between price increases and wages). The Unit also made films for other union organisations. *Bones of Building* (1956), a safety film, was commissioned by the Building Workers Industrial Union of Australia (BWIU), and *Hewers of Coal* (1957) was a film that supported a campaign for the Miner's Federation. In an attempt to put 'the real facts before the people', the films aspired to provide an alternative representation of events and issues to that of mainstream commercial media reportage.

The Unit distanced itself from traditional commercial film production companies as it was affiliated with the work of left cultural activists throughout Sydney's artistic and labour communities. The Unit provided its own production facilities, distribution and publicity. This cultural formation shared much in common with European avant-garde movements as described by Raymond Williams in his essay 'The Politics of the Avant-Garde'. These radical and alternative creative movements sought to challenge existing social orders as well as to fortify their disciplines through self-management (Williams, R. 1988, 2–14). As the Film Unit's work gained recognition throughout the labour movement, it made the decision to employ a wider range of techniques to communicate to the broader community. Norma Disher explained why, in 1956, the Unit began planning a series of animated short films:

> We were three years into our work. We were hoping that ultimately we would be sponsored not just by the wharfies, but also by the trade union movement—the ACTU—to make films for all the various unions. That was our ultimate hope. But there were times when we weren't sure that was going to happen. We also felt that when we had a bit of space, which was not often, we should try to do other things besides the documentary form … to extend our use. At the time there was a movement in the Left, particularly in the WWF, of an awareness of our indigenous people. Now this was in the '50's. There wasn't a lot going on, but there was a stirring in the Left that some focus needed to be put on the subject.
>
> (*Disher, N. 2005*, interview)

Disher, Gow and Levy maintained a collective working arrangement. Each member had great respect for the others' contributions to the filmmaking process, and they did not insist on strictly defined crew roles. The allocation of different production tasks was interdependent. Another form of collaboration involved the participation of other WWF workers in the filmmakers' practice. For their animation proposal, they approached Harry Reade because of his expertise in graphic and cartooning skills.

Reade was supportive of the Unit's work and its commitment to social justice, and he was willing to contribute to the project. He had established credentials as a versatile artist and was recognised as an accomplished cartoonist, painter and writer. His experience working on the Sydney waterfront gave him the opportunity to participate in a broad range of creative activity stimulated and supported by the WWF community. Applying himself to a variety of mediums, he also gained skills by working with significant Australian artists. From these people he learnt to adapt and integrate his strongly held political views into cultural expression. Although he had no knowledge of the process of animation, in accepting the Unit's invitation, Harry became engaged in a medium that would play an important role in his future.

NOTE

1. Formed in 1932, the New Theatre movement emerged against the background of financial and social hardships endured by wage earners during the Great Depression. Its *Agit prop* (agitational propaganda) early productions attracted a predominately working class following. From 1954 to 1968, a collaboration of actors, dramatists and wharf workers operated the New Theatre within the WWF Federal offices in Sydney.

CHAPTER 3

Wharfie Animation

In 1956, the Waterside Workers' Federation Film Unit (WWFFU) embarked on the production of a series of 25 animated short films under the title, *Land of Australia: Aboriginal Art*. The undertaking illustrated the Unit's sense of social responsibility to champion issues other than industrial conditions affecting union members. Its determination to achieve this aim reflected Greg Mallory's argument in *The Social Responsibility of Labour*, that 'progress must pay heed to the provision of social equality' (Mallory, G. 1992, 120). By endeavouring to make indigenous culture accessible to a wider audience, the Unit used independent film production to establish a relationship between local arts and otherwise marginalised cultural and social elements of the national experience. Clem Millward remembers the scant documentation of aboriginal art and SORA artists' response to it during World War II (WWII):

> The only book on aboriginal art was McCarthy's book, which was an anthropological book from the Australian Museum in Sydney. There was nothing else that I'd ever seen on aboriginal art. There was very little aboriginal painting that had been looked at as art. It had only been seen ethnologically. But some of the artists who worked

> as camoufleurs during the war ... on the airports and
> military installations around Northern Australia ...
> were very aware of aboriginal art. I know that Wallace
> Thornton brought back some beautiful pieces from
> Oenpilli'.[1] There was never any aboriginal art shown in
> galleries. The Art Gallery of NSW wouldn't have had an
> aboriginal artefact in it. They were all in the ethnographic
> section of the Museum.
>
> *(Millward, C. 2005)*

Across the Pacific during the 1920s, it was the 'ethnological' or 'primitive' art collection, at the Canterbury Museum in
Christchurch New Zealand, that influenced the creative work of
the acclaimed experimental film-maker Len Lye. Tribal artefacts
offered the avant-garde artist 'striking proof that there were powerful styles of representation that lay completely outside the traditional aesthetics of European art' (Horrocks, R. 2001, 39). Raymond
Williams makes clear the relationship between the 'primitive' and
Modernism in *The Politics of the Avant-Garde*. A striking charac-
teristic of several Modernist movements was expressed by recourse
to a more graphic art, and often drew on primitive or exotic elements of native cultures. The attraction of reaching back beyond
the existing cultural order was to rediscover a repressed native culture that had been overlain by academic and conventional forms
and formulas. Further, native art represented a broader human
tradition especially because of its supposed 'primitivist' elements, a
term which corresponded with an appreciation of the innately creative and the unformed and untamed realm of the pre-rational and
the unconscious (Williams, R. 1988, 10). Consistent with the avant-
garde's rejection of convention, Lye found in Pacific art an 'escape
route from the traditional aesthetics of European art'. Subsequently,
dot patterns in tribal totems were to become a strong motif in Lye's
art to 'convey organic life in a primary stage'.

In 1927, Lye began making sketches for the 10-minute animated film *Tusalava*. The film was inspired by the witchetty grub

totem belonging to an aboriginal tribe at Emily Gap near Alice Springs. Lye had seen photographs of the totem in F. J. Gillen and B. Spencer's *The Native Tribes of Central Australia* (1899). Eventually produced in London with the support of the London Film Society, in 1929, Roger Horrocks contends that nothing like *Tusalava* had ever been seen before:

> Unfortunately this also meant that *Tusalava* was doomed to remain isolated, for though viewers were intrigued by it, they were not sure how to talk about it or how to contextualise it.
>
> *(Horrocks, R. 2001, 90–94)*

It is unlikely that Reade, or members of the WWFFU, had seen Lye's *Tusalava*, before developing the *Land of Australia: Aboriginal Art* project. However, *Tusalava* provides a context for understanding *Land of Australia: Aboriginal Art* and its ambitions. Indeed, the recognition of indigenous art and community attitudes towards it, had changed little during the period following the 1929 release of *Tusalava* and the WWFFU's proposal in 1956. Aboriginal art remained in ethnological collections and anthropology museums to be viewed as spoils of empire, exotic curiosities or souvenirs of travel.

The focus of Lye's interest in indigenous art was in its 'clear, clean-cut, aesthetic' and what it might extract from his unconscious. He was attracted to the Modernist interest in formal aesthetic issues and the 'primitive' as a source of individual creativity. The WWFFU, on the other hand, was interested in the 'social' imperative of raising an awareness of Aboriginal culture. The WWFFU's decision to treat non-Western traditions and champion the work of indigenous peoples was a radical step in Australian society during the 1950s, for in part, it challenged the consolidated opinion regarding the primacy of Western culture. In 1950s Australia, the Aboriginal community had no voice and no vote. Australian governments had endorsed the policy of assimilation, which in practice meant that 'the destruction of Aborigines as a distinct group of people with their own culture was to be stepped up' (McQueen, H. 2004, 201). The Left was opposed to this view and supported the rebuilding and recognition of Aboriginal society. As Paddy McGuiness comments:

> One of the good things in many respects about the old communists was that they took a strong interest in aboriginal welfare. One of the best known anthropologists who went to East Germany after the Petrov Commission was Fred Rose, who became a professor at Humboldt University in East Berlin. He did quite a lot of work on aborigine anthropology. So it was very much a Left theme in those days, as it still is.
>
> (*McGuinness, P. 2005*, interview)

During the late 1930s, the Jindyworobak movement, established by Adelaide poet Rex Ingamells, called for a distinctively Australian art that would draw from 'the spirit of the land'. Ingamells espoused the movement's aims in his manifesto, *Conditional Culture*. These were to set Australian art free from 'whatever alien influences trammel it' and 'bring it into proper contact with its material' (Ingamells, R. 1938). The Jindyworobaks embraced Aboriginal culture and Anglo-Celtic Australian traditions. Their practice of turning to the stories of the Dreamtime for inspiration, and the use of aboriginal words in their poetry, led to ridicule by modernists and internationalists opposed to cultural isolationism. Subsequently, in the face of 'alien influences' that were not only steadily encroaching but also finding a receptive audience, Australia began to emerge from the 'physical and cultural cocoon' of its colonial past (Elliott, B. 1979). By the end of WWII, the movement lost much of its impetus.

Like the Jindyworobaks, the WWFFU was concerned with recognising the symbolic importance of Aboriginal culture.

However, it did not attempt to combine indigenous and white Australian symbols to tell Dreamtime stories. For the WWFFU, a political and social dimension to the project was the aim of championing the existence of a dispossessed society. In a 1956 report on films to the WWF Federal Council, WWF official, Ted Roach, advocated support for the Film Unit's proposed animated film series:

> These projects could fill a long-felt want in this country to popularise real Australian history, to help develop an appreciation of Australian culture, and assist in the recognition of the art and culture of the Aboriginal.
>
> (*Roach, T. 1956*)

In part, the WWFFU's desire to treat subject matter beyond industrial issues was driven by consideration of how to maintain funding for its expanding activities. In between live-action documentary work the Unit experienced costly lay-off periods while waiting for the production of new proposals. The animated series had the potential to alleviate financial strain and provide continuity of funded work if it could attract a market. Prospective outlets existed with 16-mm film societies, education departments and libraries. The new medium of broadcast television seemed particularly promising, as Clem Millward explains:

> It was the beginning of television in Australia and, of course, all the television programmes were made to be ten minutes short [per hour]. They had time for ads, but they also had time for short films. So the Film Unit decided they would try to make some short films not only to fill these gaps, but also to keep themselves alive, to keep the Unit alive.
>
> (*Millward, C. 2005*, interview)

In a letter to noted Australian documentary filmmaker, John Heyer, Unit member Jock Levy discussed marketing possibilities for the animation project. He was well aware of the challenge of competing with popular American cartoons, which dominated time slots on

Australian television. He wrote, 'It seems it will be difficult to find a sponsor who will risk box office receipts by backing a cartoon film which is a little different, e.g. no talking ducks or mice' (Levy, J. 1957).

The Unit members also felt that if they could access this market they might also be able to defuse some of the animosity felt towards the militant WWF by Australia's mainstream media. With the aim of averting a negative response from employer-owned and controlled media to an organisation aligned with left-wing politics, the members established a production utility called Link Films. The name 'Link' was conceived as a front that masked its association with the WWF. Jock Levy said that the name *Link* was 'just something we had to come up with so that we wouldn't put the WWF sign on it, that's all' (Levy, J. 2005, interview).

It appears that members of the Unit had little knowledge of other Australian animation studios. Certainly none served as a model for the intended projects. According to Norma Disher, the members resolved to adapt their filmmaking skills to the process of animation:

> I think we were doing it mostly to see if we could do it. I think we were trying to test our skills and see what we could do basically because we were interested in the two scenes—the Australian folk music and the indigenous peoples' legends.
>
> (*Disher, N. 2005,* interview)

DOMINANT TRENDS IN 1950s AUSTRALIAN ANIMATION

Before the introduction of television in 1956, Australian animation production was very modest in scale. It was sustained by cinema advertising, commissions and integration into documentary films. There was little focus on animated film as a medium for artistic experiment or as a platform for philosophical and social comment. Susan Dermody and Elizabeth Jacka's two volume study of Australian film, *The Screening of Australia: Anatomy of a Film Industry*, concluded that the development of Australian film was shaped by the discourses of a national cinema and commercialism (Dermody, S. and Jacka, E. 1987, 156). National film culture struggled to compete with the importation of international products that dominated Australian cinemas. Animation historian Giannalberto Bendazzi, outlines the issues that limited the development of Australian animation:

> Except for advertising the country's internal market was weak, and offered few opportunities to local animators, who turned to the much larger markets of other English speaking nations such as the United States of America and Great Britain. This, and the lack of a solid tradition, was probably the cause for the scarcity of original Australian animation, which was technically advanced but lacked a character of its own.
>
> *(Bendazzi, G. 1994, 419)*

The dominant figure of Australian animation practice in the 1950s from the 1930s was Eric Porter who, in 1931, founded Eric Porter Studios with income generated from advertising work. This provided backing for his attempts to make short children's entertainment films. Referred to as the 'Australian Disney', Porter attempted to emulate the Disney production model by implementing an assembly line system in his studio. Accordingly, he developed merchandise around *Willie the Wombat,* the central character in a 10-minute colour film *Waste Not, Want Not* made in 1939.[2] He also secured the exclusive rights for a colour film production technique, and endeavoured to improve animated film technology (Bradbury, K. 1998, 19–23).

Between 1953 and 1956, Porter tried unsuccessfully to break into the American market with three pilot films for a series—*Bimbo's Auto*[3], *Rabbit Stew* and *Bimbo's Clock*—but there was insufficient interest and none went ahead.

In the post-WWII period, political and economic relations with the United States contributed to an increase in American influence in areas of mass culture, particularly through such forms as advertising, movies, television and comics (Burn, I., et al. 1987, 137). Beginning his animation career around this time, Melbourne graphic designer and animator Alex Stitt recounted the influence of both American and European graphic design styles evident in Australian animation work:

> Apart from a general American-ness, the bibles were the *Art Directors Annual* from New York and *Graphis Annual* from Europe, in which we would see stills of the material that was happening. For example, you'd see stills of Saul Bass' film titles running in both of those publications. It was a time when American design was really dominating … ninety percent of the stuff you saw reproduced in world collections was American. It took a long time before that changed.
>
> (*Stitt, A. 2005*, interview)

Stitt also outlined the difficulties faced by local companies attempting to enter the international market, and gave a sense of the scale and type of work produced by Australian operators:

> The exhibitors were all tied to the American and English market. That part of the business was pretty hopeless. There were certainly occasional animated commercials that turned up at the cinema. The Owen Brothers had a little operation that ran for quite some years and they mostly existed on doing titling and occasional bits of animation. There were also little pockets of government utilities.
>
> (*Stitt, A. 2005*, interview)

During WWII, the Owen Brothers of Melbourne produced animated training films for the Department of Information. Their studio also made two-minute propaganda films which included *Australians Keep the Wheels of Industry Turning* (1943) and

Squander Bug (1945). The films entreated the nation not to waste economic resources and were an attempt to keep national pride and spirit buoyant. In 1953, distinguished political cartoonist and Oscar-winning independent animator Bruce Petty began work with the Owen Brothers. Commenting on his start in animation and the scale of its activity in Australia at the time, Petty observed:

> I don't think there was much. This was pre-television. The Owen Brothers used to do little PR things. We did a little road safety film for the movies.[4] I didn't know anyone else who was doing it. That's about all I did. Someone else there was working on an ad for a fridge.
>
> (*Petty, B. 2005*, interview)

The Commonwealth Scientific Investigation Research Organisation (CSIRO) Film Unit was a small government film organisation that produced educational rather than commercial films. Established in 1945, the Unit produced several titles that combined live-action with animated inserts to illustrate and explain scientific ideas. Like the WWFFU, the CSIRO Film Unit had a documentary focus and utilised animation for information purposes. Anne Jolliffe, Australia's first recognised woman animator, began her career at the Unit, gave an indication of the size and scale of its animation section in 1957:

> I was the only person there. There was a sixteen-millimetre camera—a rostrum camera—mainly because the boss there had been overseas to Disney's. And he'd decided that they [the CSIRO] should have an animation studio. I found I was animating films called *Radio Astronomy in Australia*, *Penguins of Macquarie Island*, and *The Mallee Fowl*.
>
> (*Jolliffe, A. 2005*, interview)

Despite 40 years' experience preceding the introduction of television, the Australian animation industry was very small. Collectively the studios employed few people. In 1953, the Owen

Brothers' studio comprised a total of four staff while the following year Eric Porter Studios employed seven (Bradbury, K. 1998, 27–28).

To this point, the growth of mainstream Australian animation had been shaped by its association with the advertising, art and cartoon industries. Its 'model for narrative techniques, technological innovations, production processes and commercial strategies' were informed largely by animation in the United States. The desire (or perhaps need) to emulate American rivals and to compete in the international arena also often encouraged the dilution or disappearance of antipodean content (Bradbury, K. 1998, 208). Moreover, Australian animation was not renowned for the power of its social or political commentary. Its priority, during this time, was focussed on animated cartoons for mass entertainment, particularly for children.

Whether or not the WWFFU was aware of what was happening at the time in Australian animation, it had very different imperatives and would follow its own path. Reade empathised with the Unit's focus on animation as a vehicle for public education and took the opportunity to engage with the medium as a vehicle through which to inject the spirit of his ideological convictions.

THE WATERSIDE WORKERS' FEDERATION FILM UNIT AND ANIMATION

Operating outside the constraints of the local industry, the WWFFU model differed on several fronts from the production conventions and narrative model of film produced by contemporary Australian animation studios. Technologically, it used rudimentary equipment and 16-mm film rather than the 35-mm format; institutionally, it maintained a communal working arrangement as opposed to a corporate structure; economically, its prime motivation was to educate rather than make a profit; and politically, it explored marginal subjects and disenfranchised culture rather than focusing on mainstream entertainment.

LAND OF AUSTRALIA: ABORIGINAL ART

Bohra, the Kangaroo and Wyamba the Turtle

The *Land of Australia: Aboriginal Art* project was born out of Jock Levy's interest in stories based on aboriginal legends which he viewed as ideal subject matter for an animated series (Levy, J. 2005, interview). Unit members Disher and Gow agreed and they selected two narratives, *Bohra, the kangaroo* and *Wyamba, the turtle*, to begin the Link venture. *Bohra, the kangaroo* is a tribal myth explaining why the day is divided into periods of light and dark, while *Wyamba, the turtle* tells the story of how the turtle got its shell.

During the pre-production stage, they collaborated with Peter Hamilton of Wattle Recording Company, which had been collecting and popularising Australian folk songs. Through Hamilton the Unit sought advice and access to the original recordings of aboriginal music held by Professor Adolphus Peter 'A P' Elkin from the Anthropology Department at Sydney University. Harry Reade was then recruited to do the drawings. Clem Millward remembered that Harry was already 'conscious of aspects of aboriginal art', having designed a leaflet-poster based on aboriginal motifs for the EYL in 1949. Harry was enthusiastic about applying his graphic and cartooning ability to animation and, in his first attempt, proved to be particularly adept at the medium. His trial-and-error approach resulted in a technique that was quick, effective and cheap to produce. As Clem Millward recalled:

> It was out of those simple forms that Harry thought up his process. Harry designed it. Harry made it. He wanted to make these animated films and he worked it out … he may have got it out of a book somewhere but … he made the board for fitting his cels [celluloid sheets] onto, he invented all of the characters, he designed the whole thing, he drew all of the animation sequences. All his drawings were done on cels and my contribution was the backgrounds and

titles. Harry did all the actual animation. Norma, Jock Levy and Keith Gow did the actual filming of it. Harry wasn't involved in the stop-motion photography part of it.

(*Millward, C. 2005,* interview)

The graphic design and simple movements depicted in *Land of Australia: Aboriginal Art* reflects the style of work produced by the small revolutionary American animation studio, United Productions of America (UPA) whose style fused animation techniques with innovative currents in graphics and plastic arts. Indeed, the studio launched a vocabulary for animation which married modernist concerns with cartoons. Rather than use the detailed graphic naturalism associated with the work of the Disney studio, UPA utilised designs based on simplified line, abstract backgrounds, flat fields of colour and collage. The studio's use of fewer drawings than conventional full animation also generated a stylistic form known as 'limited animation' (Klein, N. M. 1993, 229–249).

Clem Millward was of the opinion that the WWFFU's film design and style of motion may have also been influenced by that of East European animation. The WWF hall had been a venue for weekly screenings, and the programmes enabled audiences to see works outside British and American distribution, many coming from the Soviet Union and East European nations. Animated cartoons from these countries accompanied the usual fare of documentaries and feature films. A common element in the animated works was the development of 'the technique of limited animation, which saved time, work and money while experimenting with a 'new' style. This trend in East European animation was similar to the one pursued by the American UPA a few years earlier' (Bendazzi, G. 1994, 171). Millward claimed that this style was important to Reade because it provided him with a model of animation that suited his graphic ability.

Harry used line, shape, colour and moving graphic symbols to represent the essence of the two aboriginal legends. The character designs clearly reference the flat two-dimensional graphic styles of indigenous ancestral spirit drawings. In general, movement was achieved using an animation technique known as 'filmograph' which infused still images with the illusion of movement by means of optical effects, camera zooms and pans over still images. The process had established itself as an inexpensive form of animation commonly used in educational and industrial films. These often relied on constructing cinematic narratives out of movements over photographs. Reade embellished this technique by adding limited stop-motion effects which were achieved by directly drawing with oil pastels under the camera and recording sequential advancements of the line.

The WWFFU operated in a section of the top floor room of the 60–66 Sussex Street building. Lack of appropriate space for a dark-room prompted the Unit to use the building's dark, musty, dirt-floored basement which could only be reached by ladder through a trap door in the ground floor. This space offered enough head height to set up lighting and an artwork stand, giving new meaning to the term 'underground'.

The Unit's simple production methods did not require the costly features of theatrical animation. Reade's recollection of the 16-mm camera mount and the artwork support base indicated just how elementary the WWFFU's facilities were compared to the robust professional rigs which were designed and constructed to accommodate controlled and precise movements. The Unit's camera was mounted on a table sitting on roller skates running between two lengths of angle iron. The set-up facilitated sequential, incremental movement of the camera either towards or away from the artwork which was fixed to a sliding aluminium framed window mounted vertically at one end of the basement (Bannah, M. 1997). Keith Gow, who had researched cinema techniques, helped Harry understand the rudimentary filming process he had adapted. On Gow's uncomplicated shooting procedure, Jock Levy added:

> We set up in the most simple way. But not only was it simple, it was effective because of Keith's technique,

like waving the bloody drawings in front of the camera to get the effect of an aboriginal battle. Keith was very clever.

(Levy, J. 2005)

The Unit worked on a tight budget with members working for wages and no funding in the accepted meaning of the term. Harry worked in a 'voluntary' capacity because he approved of the cause and the question of money was not even raised:

We were very resourceful. All our work was done with a Bolex camera … we were extremely conscious that we were using the union member's money and our ethics were that you don't waste that money.

(Disher, N. 2005, interview)

On its release in 1957, *Land of Australia: Aboriginal Art* appealed to both national and international audiences. It was screened to a variety of audiences, including at the 1957 Sydney Film

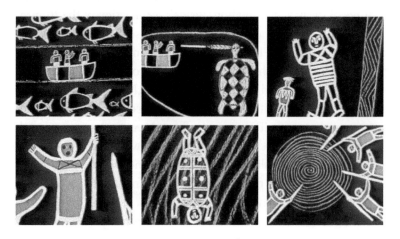

FIGURE 3.1 Still frames from *Land of Australia: Aboriginal Art: Wyamba, the Turtle* (1956) animated by Harry Reade. (Courtesy of the Maritime Union of Australia.)

Festival, the Sydney Film Society and the Sydney University Film Group. Copies of the film were purchased by the Visual Education Centres in Sydney for use in NSW schools. It was screened at the Tenth Jubilee International Film Festival in Czechoslovakia and also at the 1957 Edinburgh Film Festival. A copy was sent to Michael Balcon at Ealing Films in the United Kingdom, who reported that 'in my view the treatment is attractive, particularly for specialised audiences' (Milner, L. 2003, 99–100).

In 1978, the Aboriginal Arts Board commissioned the Sydney-based animation studio, Air Programs International (API), to produce 'a series of works … designed to give Aborigines and Europeans a better understanding of the Aboriginal Dreamtime culture' (Mendham, T. and K. Hepper 1978, 56). One of the titles, *Dreamtime, This Time, Dreamtime: The Aboriginal Children's History of Australia*, was the second film to meet with the Australian Broadcasting Control Board's (ABCB) definition of wholly 'Australian'; that is broadcast material 'produced by Australians for Australians and about Australian history and culture' (Harrison, K. 1980, 43). The first to satisfy the ABCB's 'Australian' criteria was Yoram Gross's animated feature, *Dot and the Kangaroo* (1977). It is significant therefore that, 20 years earlier, with its production of *Bohra, the kangaroo* and *Wyamba, the turtle*, the WWFFU had foreshadowed the aim of the Aboriginal Arts Board when it used animation to project Aboriginal art and culture.

'Click Go the Shears'

Link's follow-up animated film was *Click Go the Shears*, a project inspired by a stage production. Following its premiere at the Melbourne New Theatre in March 1953, Dick Diamond's classic musical *Reedy River* contributed to a revival of interest in Australian folk culture. Set in an outback shearing shed during the Great Shearer's Strike of 1891, the show celebrated the rise of the labour movement and the birth of the Australian Labor Party. Taking its name from Henry Lawson's poem of the same name, the stage production was built around bush ballads and songs from the period.

Norma Disher, who had been active in Sydney's New Theatre along with Levy and Gow, recalled that through *Reedy River* Diamond had created 'this experience that brought in our shearers and it was loaded with wonderful tunes that everybody could sing—this incredible bush music'.

Following the end of WWII, Australia experienced prolonged economic growth and a growing sense of optimism. It was now surrounded by newly independent Asian countries and Britain had been dislodged as its most important trading market. A massive immigration program had brought in migrants from around the globe. In this changing world, Australians sought 'cohesion, balance and confidence'. The bushman was affirmed as the authentic Australian character. Old stereotypes were reclaimed through stories, poems and songs, which intimately linked the roots of Australian labourism with Australian nationalism (Day, D. 1998, 84–87). Much of the appeal of folk music for the Left was the focus the subject of the songs put on elements of national culture. The device of reaching back beyond the existing order to interpret national icons associated with the labour movement had important cultural and political dimensions. In *The Politics of the Avant-Garde,* Raymond Williams outlines the appeal and vitality of 'folk' art:

> The 'folk' emphasis, when offered as evidence of a repressed popular tradition, could move readily towards socialist and other radical and revolutionary tendencies … the vitality of the naïve could be joined with this, as witness of the new kinds of art which a popular revolution would release.
>
> (*Williams, R. 1988,* 10)

In 1950, Vance Palmer, a leading advocate of Australian literary nationalism, published a collection of *Old Australian Bush Ballads.* Palmer's aim was 'to make a songbook that could be used in a popular way, thus preserving contact with the simple, democratic tradition of campfire and track that is one part of our inheritance' (Palmer, V. 1950). The WWFFU shared this philosophy and enthusiastically grasped the opportunity to make its contribution to Australian folk culture with the animated film *Click Go the Shears*.

The lyrics of *Click Go the Shears* captures the atmosphere of a busy shearing shed in full swing. Shearers had played an important role in introducing unionism to Australia and wharfies empathised with the militancy and socialisation of pastoral workers. The more skilful among the shearers were an elite group among the shed hands of rouseabouts, washers and pressers. In the days of manual cutting blades, the man who sheared the most sheep was known as the 'ringer'. He also collected the biggest cheque.

Harry Reade and Clem Millward shared the preparation of artwork for *Click Go the Shears*. Harry designed and animated the foreground figures on celluloid overlays and Clem Millward painted the static background panels. The sound track is a recording of the song by Cedric McLaughlin and the Link Singers. Reade's design for the production utilised loose, broken outlines to define characters and flat broad brush strokes that suggested background forms. Areas of colour crossed over without scrupulously following the outlines of these forms. The visual style and minimalist animation (in part dictated by the rudimentary production conditions), was an extension of the approach established in the earlier films. The illusion of movement was achieved using stop-motion recordings of alternate pose drawings. In each case the essence of a character's action was constructed using just two drawings that were aligned using an elementary two-hole stationery punch registration system. The first illustrated the beginning or one extreme of an action, and the second captured the completion of that action. For example, a shearer holding a sheep was drawn with his arm raised as if to begin clipping wool. A second drawing depicted the arm and shears at the end of the cutting

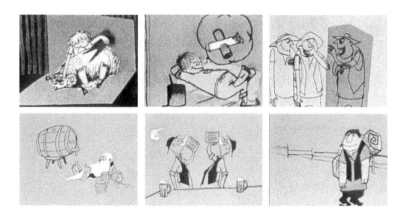

FIGURE 3.2   Still frames from Click Go the Shears (1956) animated by Harry Reade and Clem Millward. (Courtesy of the Maritime Union of Australia.)

stroke. The cyclic recording of these two drawings achieved the illusion of the shearer's repetitive work (Figure 3.2).

The 16-mm film was screened to small groups such as the Sydney University Film Group and a Melbourne film society group which described the film as 'one of the successes of the film weekend' (General Reviews. 1958, 22). When attempts to find a distributor for the animated films were unsuccessful, the Film Unit reconsidered its position, disbanded Link Films and shifted its focus to the production of union sponsored live-action films.

'Four's a Crowd'

In 1957, Harry's final contribution to the work of the WWFFU was to a 14-minute black and white live-action comedy, *Four's a Crowd*. Wharfies were derided by the media as strike-prone loafers and heavy drinkers, and as Norma Disher explained, the film presented four different types of WWF members whose habits and behaviour were regularly attacked by an antagonistic mainstream press:

> The film consisted of four vignettes, which illustrated the slap-stick performances of four wharfie types who would

probably be considered not the ideal members of a gang because they were slightly recalcitrant in some way. Jock Levy acted in the film to portray the role of each character—Glass-Arm Harry, Tiddly Pete, Nick-Away Ned, and Ron the Roaster.

(Disher, N. 2005, interview)

The film was an instructive tale that defended the union's reputation and sought to improve the attitudes of workers. The behaviour of each character was portrayed as having a negative effect on members, their jobs and their union. Harry's cartoon interpretations of the lead characters were integrated into the title sequence which included the caption: 'any similarity between persons portrayed in this film and *real* persons is no coincidence'.

THE END OF THE WWFFU

The work of the WWFFU came to an end in 1958. The effects of automation had led to a drop in WWF membership and a simultaneous lack of funding to support the Film Unit. The changing priorities of the labour movement and its lack of co-operation with the militant WWF also took a toll. In addition, the effects of suburbanisation drew wharfies and their families away from the inner city. The appeal of travelling from distant suburbs to events in the Branch Hall also diminished with the introduction of television in 1956. Economic growth and developing consumerism added to an emphasis on the role of the individual over the group. All of these issues contributed to the demobilisation of the Film Unit, which had done so much to represent the values of the WWF on film. During its five years of operation it had produced and screened its work to union members and film groups on a non-profit basis. When the Unit was challenged by the WWF leadership to become a profit-making business concern and the ACTU did not take the opportunity to administer the unit on behalf of the trade union movement, its work ended (Milner, L. 2003, 77–79).

Milner has argued that the WWFFU played a positive role in empowering a team of working-class people to create their own cultural forms. At the very least it gave WWF members a 'voice' to express their concerns. It brought into focus a number of social, political and economic injustices that were perpetrated by a capitalist structure. However, by the 1950s, improvements in working and living conditions led to a decline in the notion of class distinctiveness in Australian society. This change also had its effect on the organised left and the CPA.

A different concept of class was developing that focused more on income, consumption and living standards, all of which drew attention away from the problems that still existed in Australia. The WWFFU films challenged many truisms of life in Sydney in the 1950s and they contradicted the decade's powerful myth of conformity. They showed ways in which Australia was not 'the lucky country': it was not luck, but the capitalist system that created inequality (Milner, L. 2003, 123–126).

Although the demise of the WWFFU brought Harry's participation in animation in Australia to an end, it had given him the opportunity to discover the possibilities of a new medium. Animation connected his illustration and cartooning skills with the collaborative practice of social commitment through cultural expression. Commenting on Reade's contribution to the WWFFU, Norma Disher stated:

> As far as the WWFFU is concerned, Harry made a very valuable contribution. In fact we couldn't have made *Click go the Shears* and *Aboriginal Art* without him … I think the drawings he did were quite beautiful, especially for the 'legends'. Harry was quite a difficult person to work with but on the 'legends' he seemed to be extremely enthusiastic and most cooperative.
>
> (*Disher, N. 2005*, interview)

THE SYDNEY PUSH

Reade continued to draw cartoons for *Tribune* while he worked as a museum attendant repairing deteriorating specimens for the Natural History Museum at Sydney University. This position appeared to offer temporary relief only, as he was still determined to participate in social and political change. He wrote in his unpublished manuscript:

> As a young man it led me to the ranks of those who sought to change society on a grand scale then, as hope for change faded, to spend time with those who often acted as though society didn't exist at all. The equivalent of America's beat generation sans chic ... the last of the bohemians, the first of the hippies ... to those who were all of these and none of these ... The Push.
>
> (*Reade, H. 1998*)

The Sydney Push was a congregation of freethinkers who operated from the late 1940s to the 1970s in downtown Sydney pub culture. Some members of the group were associated with the Sydney Libertarian Society and some were followers of John Anderson, Professor of Philosophy at Sydney University (1927–1958). The distinctive features of the Libertarian philosophy, outlined in 1975 by A. J. Baker in *The Sydney Libertarians Broadsheet*, were support for empiricism and objective enquiry, and the rejection of religion, conventional morality and censorship. Anderson also promoted 'permanent criticism'. Push members engaged in the critique of morality and used argument to expose its illusions. The group espoused an unsentimental approach to life and members were generally atheists, supporters of sexual freedom and opponents of repressive institutions. Followers reacted against just about every social and political demand of every field of human activity. James Franklin's essay,

The Push and Political Drinkers, describes the appeal of the Push to the Left during the late 1950s and early 1960s:

> The urge for youthful rebellion that provided some of the motivation for seeking out the Push would in earlier years have been satisfied by joining the Communist Party. But the demise of Communism in splits and its discrediting after Hungary and Khrushchev's speech on the horrors of Stalinism meant that by the early 1960s there was little appeal in traditional left-wing politics. With the Communists marginalised and Labor split, the Push to some extent filled an ideological vacuum.
>
> *(Franklin, J. 1953)*

According to Paddy McGuinness, Reade empathised with the Push's rejection of conformism and critique of authority. He was not amenable to being told what to do and 'couldn't stand attempts to discipline him'. He was 'happier with the quasi-anarchism of the Push' and thus frequently moved in their circles (McGuinness, P. 2005, interview). However, while Reade had an anarchist streak and enjoyed the company and stimulation of Push members, he was also attracted to political activism. His opposition to the capitalist system did not mean that he opposed all systems, and his continued support for an alternative political ideology was considered by Push members as 'romantic leftism'.

On 1 January 1959, popular Cuban support for Fidel Castro's revolutionary forces led to the overthrow the US-backed regime of General Fulgencio Batista. Batista fled to the Dominican Republic and Castro set out to establish Cuba as a socialist state. This included the fundamental transformation of social and economic state apparatuses and a ban on all forms of private enterprise. The new government introduced agrarian and urban reform that included expropriating the property of all large landowners and nationalising all large enterprises.

In 1960, Castro appealed to international unions for support to overcome problems facing the Revolution. The request triggered discussion within Push circles and stirred Reade into action. He states in *An Elephant Charging My Chookhouse* that reading the slogan *Territorio Libre de Analfabetismo* (Territory free of Illiteracy) supporting Cuba's drive to make reading and writing universal on an island with a high rate of illiteracy, fuelled his desire to assist. In an interview given to the communist newspaper *Hoy* in 1962, Reade said that on 2 January 1961, he read the Cuban Revolutionary Government's call to the world for support against a planned foreign attack and that this was an 'unforgettable day' for him when he made the decision to buy a ticket to Cuba and fight for the Revolution (Alfonso, C. 1962). His friend Pat Evans confirmed Harry's urge for action and his ability to act in accordance with his own form of dissent:

> He was one of only twenty or thirty people in Sydney—
> some of them were wharfies, some of them were members
> of the Push—who'd sat around and talked about going to
> Cuba. He was the only one who went because he reckoned
> that he put his money where his mouth was.
>
> (*Evans, P. 2005,* interview)

The disinclination of Reade's circle of friends to act in support of Cuba's new regime is explained by Franklin who points out that apart from a general emphasis on 'criticism', the Push as a movement lacked 'activism':

> While they were against the State, they had no intention
> of provoking it, or working towards its downfall. Much
> less did they expect it to change. Demonstrating in the
> streets or organising for political action was regarded as
> succumbing to illusions.
>
> (*Franklin, J. 1953*)

In February 1961, Reade departed from Sydney aboard the vessel S.S. Willem Ruys, armed with introductions provided by the Eureka Youth League and several left-wing trade unions prepared to facilitate his entry into Cuba (ASIO. Henry Garbutt Reade. File 39). At 33 years of age, he took with him the imprint of his restless, wandering upbringing and a commitment to the class struggle that had brought him into conflict with his community's dominant ideological system. His working class background and self-education had shaped him as a resourceful person who could go it alone. He had an anarchist streak and didn't fear authority. He was accomplished in the creative skills of writing, painting, cartooning and animation. Each of these activities had shaped his attempts to link cultural expression with political struggle. As a creative citizen, the opportunity to participate in the excitement of a society's revolutionary transformation from capitalism to communism, was one to which he was eager to commit. He also carried with him a 16-mm print of the film he had animated—*Land of Australia: Aboriginal Art.*

NOTES

1. Oenpelli is a region in Western Arnhem Land in the Northern Territory. The traditional subjects of Aboriginal bark paintings from the region, relate to the plants, animals and natural phenomena significant to Kunwinjka culture.
2. *Waste Not, Want Not* had a musical score written by Lance Watkinson which included the theme song, 'I'm Willie the Wombat'. This song was a popular success and sheet music for it sold for 2s. There was also a *Willie the Wombat* colouring book—50,000 copies each of which were sold through Woolworths and Coles for 9d (Bertrand, I. ed. 1989).
3. Bradbury, K. (1998) outlines the striking similarities between the narratives of Porter's *Bimbo's Auto* (1954) and Disney's *Little Susie Blue Coupe* (1953).
4. *Careful Koala* (1953)—a community awareness film for children about the dangers of road traffic, produced by the Owen Brothers and animated by Bruce Petty.

CHAPTER 4

Our Man in Havana

Harry Reade arrived in Cuba on 23 February 1961. To avoid questioning by Australian authorities about his intentions in a socialist state he 'falsified' his travel documents by indicating that his final destination was Balbao, Panama (ASIO. Henry Garbutt Reade. File 39). In Havana, he presented himself to the People's Socialist Party—a member group of the Revolutionary Government's Integrated Revolutionary Organisations (ORI). He volunteered his creative skills to the service of the Revolution and was offered work as a cartoonist for the Cuban Communist Party's newspaper *Hoy* (Padrón, J. 2006b, interview). In an article published in *Hoy* in 1962, Reade emphasised his commitment to the Revolution and its policy of educating children and combating illiteracy:

> He wanted to put his art to the service of the working class, where he could be most useful. He wanted to offer the country through his work those fantastic things, which make the Revolution. [Reade said], 'My projects? To go to the Sierra Maestra to work as a volunteer; to go where the Revolution designates me; to participate and use art to educate children and shake their patriotic

spirit.' He wanted to make works that reflect the struggles of the working class.

(*Alfonso, C. 1962*)

In the wake of the 1959 Revolution, relations between Cuba and the United States of America were strained. Castro's revolutionary government had initiated economic reforms that focused on national development. A series of basic laws changed the semi-colonial nature of Cuba's capitalist structure. The Nationalisation Decree of October 1960 introduced a campaign proclaiming the expropriation without indemnification of national and foreign industries. More than 80 percent of the means of production and basic processes came under the control of the new State. These policies threatened the profits and land holdings of US businesses and individuals, which in turn prompted a hostile reaction from the US Government. In March 1960, President Eisenhower authorised the Central Intelligence Agency (CIA) to initiate a plan titled *A Program of Covert Action against the Castro Regime.* A force of Cuban exiles, committed to ousting Castro, was recruited and trained by the CIA in southern Florida and Guatemala.

When diplomatic relations between the United States and Cuba were broken on 3 January 1961, the Rebel Army mobilised the Cuban people. It created militia groups and instigated military and civil defence training. On 17 April 1961, with the approval of newly inaugurated US President John F. Kennedy, a US-sponsored counter-revolutionary force stormed the beaches of Playa Larga and Playa Girón on the southern coast of Cuba at the Bahia de Cochinos (*Bay of Pigs*). This attempt to oust Castro was crushed in two days by the Rebel Army and the People's Militia. The failure of the invasion humiliated the Kennedy administration and provided Castro with a significant victory with which to rally the people of Cuba. The United States retaliated with a trade embargo and withdrew all technical assistance and aid.

After arriving in Cuba, Reade enlisted in the Brigada Internacional—a militia unit comprised of foreign volunteers. The unit was ready to fight when the enemy began bombing Cuban airfields on 15 April 1961. According to Cuba's foremost animator Juan Padrón, one of Reade's first drawings in Cuba was a black lithographic crayon drawing on militia blue paper, which he produced for a 'Fight for your Country' poster. It depicted a militia man running into battle looking back over his shoulder and encouraging others to follow. At a 1996 public lecture, Reade explained that the Cuban forces were reluctant to allow the brigade of international volunteers to be exposed to enemy fire, but *he* was keen for action. He was a robust individual who was unafraid of physical confrontation, but he also believed that if international volunteers took a stand it would deliver to the world a message of support for the legitimacy of the Revolution. He angrily demanded that the unit be sent to the frontline to engage with the invading forces—'to show the oppressor that Cuba does not stand alone' (Bannah, M. 1997). The Rebel Army, however, held the International Brigade back until the invading force had been successfully repelled at the Bay of Pigs. It then sent the unit to the front to help secure the region of Playa Girón. In a July 1961 article published in the Australian *Tribune*, Reade reported on his participation in support of Castro's army:

> I was in Havana during the bombings…. I was also at Playa Girón and (coincidence) the 'Central Australia' sugar mill, on the last day of the war. My experiences during that 24 hours will stay with me for the rest of my life … the filthy cynicism of the prisoners was in sharp contrast with the fantastic morale of the militia. Believe me, they (the Cuban people) are making history; elimination of illiteracy in one year for a starter. I met Fidel Castro … Che Guevara, Minister for Economics, is a wonder. Every Sunday he's a wharfie or a builders' labourer or something.
>
> (*Reade, H. 1961, 7*)

Following the Bay of Pigs incident, Reade resumed working for *Hoy* as a political cartoonist. He also applied his skills to the improvement of traditional Cuban work practices. At the behest of Blas Roca, one of the founders of the Cuban Marxist-Leninist party, he made a study of Australian sugarcane harvesting methods and how they could be applied in Cuba. At the time, the burning of cane fields in Cuba was considered a treasonable act as Cubans were terrified of the fires caused by US air attacks that were designed to destroy the sugar harvest. Reade based much of his study on the knowledge he had gained from one of his many itinerant jobs—cutting cane in Australia. The results of his research along with drawings, layouts and a wooden model of an Australian cane-knife were shown to just a few party heads then quickly put aside (Tanner, H. 2006, interview).

In a feature article *Harry Reade Y Sus Dibujos (Harry Reade and his drawings)* published in the 1 April 1962 edition of *Hoy,* Reade related the influences on his life and the events that led him to actively support the revolution. At the time, he had become one of *Hoy's* three editorial cartoonists. Several examples of his Cuban work illustrate the article. The influence of the School of Realist Art (SORA) is apparent in his style. It marries realism and caricature to directly illustrate themes. Each drawing rendered in charcoal and pen outline depicts an imposing figure dominating the vulnerable.

The larger figures captured in bold gestures threaten smaller characters or groups. The relationship between the figures contributes to the expression of strong anti-imperialist themes. Reade has accentuated the vulnerability of the smaller figures by rendering them with a finer, more fragile line. The composition of the figures in each drawing develops about a strong eyeline or axis that directly links the domineering with the powerless. The cartoons differ somewhat from his earlier Australian *Tribune* work, which generally relied on text or Australian colloquialisms to clarify the subject matter. This development in Reade's cartoons likely stemmed from his attempt to overcome language barriers. The *Hoy* cartoons succeed in communicating their message through bold visual strategies rather than a dependence on dialogue or text.

PARTICIPATING IN THE NATIONAL LITERACY CAMPAIGN

At the beginning of 1961, more than 1 million Cubans in a population of 7.29 million were illiterate. The Revolutionary government declared 1961 'The Year of Education' and initiated the *Campaña de Alfabetización*, a national literacy campaign. It set in action the mass mobilisation of 280,000 volunteer workers including many secondary school students, deemed to be literacy *brigadistas*, who taught Cuban peasants how to read and write. The motto of the campaign was 'If you know, teach; if you don't know, learn'. In April 1961, while addressing campaign volunteers departing from Vardareo, Castro said:

> You are going to teach, but as you teach, you will also learn. You are going to learn much more than you can possibly teach ... because while you teach them what you have learned in school, they will be teaching you what they have learned from the hard life that they have led. They will teach you the 'why' of the revolution better than any speech, better than any book.
>
> (Keeble, A. 2001)

Reade appreciated the role that literature had played in his own intellectual development and was keen to participate in the campaign. Within months of arriving in Cuba, he had acquired an elementary knowledge of the Spanish language and joined the brigade of volunteers.

A Cuban Ministry of Education magazine *El Mundo De La Educación* (*The World of Education*) acknowledged Harry's contribution to the campaign in an article titled, 'An Australian Who Teaches the Alphabet: A Peculiar Case of Enthusiasm and Cooperation—A Cartoonist Who Left Australia in Answer to the Call of Fidel' (Hoy, 1 April 1962). Harry illustrated the magazine cover and stated that his visits to the Sierra Maestra region had taught him much about aspects of the Revolution and had 'increased his interest in cooperating with it'. During the campaign, he used his drawing skills to support his teaching methods (ASIO. Henry Garbutt Reade. Files 81, 83).

On 12 July 1961 while the literacy campaign was underway, an article published in *Tribune* included an appeal by the Eureka Youth League for readers to support a worldwide campaign called *One Million Pencils for Cuba*. The aim of which was 'to assist the conquest of Cuba's illiteracy' (*Tribune*. 1961b, 10). Four months later, another article in *Tribune* announced that 'the first Cuban films to come out of Cuba since the Revolution' would be screened by the EYL at the Waterside Workers' Federation Hall in Sussex Street. The films were on loan to the EYL for the part they had played in collecting more than 10,000 pencils for the young people of Cuba (*Tribune*. 1961a, 11). It is unclear whether Reade initiated the Australian appeal but given his former involvement with the EYL and the WWF Sydney Branch as well as his correspondence with *Tribune*, it is probable that he was responsible.

On 22 December 1961, thousands of volunteer teachers in Havana's Revolutionary Square celebrated the reduction of the nation's illiteracy rate, which was purported to have fallen from 23 to 4 percent in the space of one year. Castro declared that Cuba was now a 'Territory Free of Illiteracy' and announced 'an end to four centuries of ignorance'. The literacy campaign had also raised the capacity of Cubans to fully engage in the arts and culture. For Reade, the success of the operation reflected the egalitarianism present in the Revolutionary government's social policy. It was a positive enactment of his ideological beliefs. As an individual he had been able to contribute to the collective to make a difference in society, and the fact that this could be done reinforced his commitment 'to participate and use art to educate children'.

1961 was an extremely active year for Reade as he applied his creative skills to help realise the Revolution's social projects. He became an illustrator for the publishing house Editorial Gente NuevA (Publishing New People) which specialised in publications for children; he designed and made puppets for the newly created national children's theatre Guiñol Infantil De Cuba in Havana; and he wrote and sent up-to-date articles about the Revolution to Australian newspapers (Padrón, J. 2004, interview).

Harry's reports merged personal experience with dramatic events. As an active participant in the Revolution he followed in the tradition of American writers John Reed and Ernest Hemingway. Reed's 'participatory journalism' described events of the Mexican Revolution between 1913 and 1914 and the 1919 Bolshevik Revolution in Russia, and likewise Hemingway described the events of the Spanish Civil War in 1936.

ICAIC AND THE ESTABLISHMENT OF ESTUDIOS CUBANACÁN

On 20 March 1959, three months after the Revolution began, the Cuban Government created a state film institute, the Instituto Cubano del Arte e Industria Cinematográficos (Cuban Institute of the Art and Industry of Cinema—ICAIC). Alfredo Guevara, a young activist in the urban underground that had supported the guerrillas and a comrade of Castro's from student days, was appointed to head the new unit. Recognising film's potential to stimulate radical cultural consciousness, ICAIC focused on cultural-specific representations of Cuban reality. This emphasis was intended to counter the influence of foreign films screened in Cuban cinemas.

Calling the motion picture medium 'a tool of the Revolution', Castro charged the Institute with the task of making movies that served the interests of the new state and its people. Moreover, it was entrusted with 'the most direct and extensive vehicle for education and the popularisation of ideas' (Agramonte, A. 1996, 116). ICAIC defended the Revolution with its own weekly newsreel programme, *Noticiero ICAIC*. The documentary was given precedence over fictional subjects because ICAIC held the belief that this genre dealt with truth more directly than fictional films and were thus better suited to raising the revolutionary awareness of the masses (Schroeder, P. A. 2002, 3). Julianne Burton has explained that both economic and ideological factors motivated the preference for the documentary form:

> The economic motivations are obvious: when funds and equipment are limited, professional actors, elaborate scripts, costuming, as studio sets can be regarded as non-essentials. [Moreover], in a society which subscribes to the principles of Marxism-Leninism, it is believed fitting that creative activity be based on the confrontation with material reality.
>
> (*Burton, J. 1997,* 126)

Despite the strong support for documentary production, ICAIC's cultural-specific representations of reality embraced all forms of cinema, including fiction and animation. When television was introduced into Cuba in 1950, the relatively small population of 5 million was serviced by five black and white broadcast channels. In 1958, a colour channel was added. During this period, commercial production serviced the needs of Cuban television and supported the establishment of several small independent animation studios. In 1959 when ICAIC was founded, a small department of cartoon animation already existed in Publicitaria Siboney, an advertising agency in Havana. It produced black and white commercials for Cuban television as well as some Latin American countries. In charge of the department's scriptwriting and designs were Jesús de Armas, an animator, and Eduardo Muñoz Bachs, an outstanding illustrator and graphic designer. In June 1959, they were joined by a young animation enthusiast, Hernán Henriquez, who had completed a Californian 'How to Animate' correspondence course, and impressed De Armas and Muñoz Bachs with his speed and skills. Together they made a 3-min animated film, *La Prensa Seria* (*The Serious Press*), a political satire directed at adults which they hoped would persuade Guevara to consider animation as part of ICAIC's service. The film denounced 'the slanders and lies published by the private press and emphasised the need to keep it under control' (Cobas, R. 1984, 110) and by its conclusion, the central character's attitude changes from scepticism to belief in the Revolution.

La Prensa Seria succeeded in convincing Guevara that animation had the potential to make an effective contribution to ICAIC's aims. In December 1959, Guevara authorised the creation of Dibujos Animados ICAIC (Animated Cartoons ICAIC) and invited them to join it. Almost 50 years later, the noted Cuban journalist and art critic Pedro de la Hoz was to vindicate Guevara's decision to establish a studio in which artistic innovation would seek to coexist with political and social struggle: 'What's most important is that with animation and other graphic media ... we have an extraordinary weapon for the formation and transmission of revolutionary, patriotic and human values, and for cultivating the sensitivity, love and intelligence needed to help us conquer the future' (Stock, A. 2009, 126).

Despite De Armas, Muñoz Bachs and Henriquez being offered reduced wages and an animation unit that lacked materials and equipment, they left Siboney Advertising with the belief that through the new unit 'they saw the future' (Tejeda, W. W. 2005). The first animated short film they produced was *El Maná* (1960)[1], 'a film about land reform in Cuba, made in the UPA style' (Zagury, L. 1999).

ICAIC's small animation department soon attracted artists, designers and even young students of theatre interested in utilising the medium and developed into a dynamic cultural centre made up of diverse creative disciplines. As the nationalisation of industries proceeded, the Government set up the Bank of Foreign Commerce to function as a foreign-trade agency. It had instructions to import large quantities of goods as rapidly as possible in order to reduce the impact of an anticipated embargo by the United States (Chanan, M. 2004, 129). ICAIC thus acquired the latest animation equipment including the world's foremost animation rostrum stand from Oxberry. By 1962, the unit outgrew its allocated space on the third floor of the Atlantic Building in

El Vedado. To accommodate the steady increase in animation production and recognising the need for improved equipment and facilities, the Government built spacious new premises dedicated to the needs of the department—Estudios Cubanacán—in a neighbourhood on the outskirts of Havana.

ICAIC documentary films made during the 1960s fell into three groups. The first comprised didactic films aimed at farmers. These dealt with topics such as agricultural methods, handling drinking water and the formation of cooperatives, schools and other facilities. The second group recorded the government's principal mass mobilisations to defend the Revolution. The third group included films that dealt with the revolutionary process, or aspects of Cuba's social and cultural history (Chanan, M. 2004, 129).

As the director of Estudios Cubanacán, Jesús de Armas influenced the mode and content of its early works. According to Tulio Raggi, one of ICAIC's notable animation directors, De Armas favoured the exploration of the revolutionary process through experimental animation that dealt with aspects of Cuba's social and cultural history. De Armas had spent four months in the United States where he had met Stephen Bosustow, one the founders of UPA. Bosustow exposed him to UPA's creative methods and he passed this knowledge on to fellow Cuban animators. De Armas also looked to innovation in design and thematic intent. Paco Prats, an ICAIC producer, claimed that, 'in the sixties we discovered a new world and we put all our spirit into it. We wanted to explore all the languages [of animation] and take the time to create our own ways'. To this end, Dibujos Animados ICAIC embraced an organisational method for personnel that had been successful in Poland, Czechoslovakia and the Soviet Union. Members were organised into 'creative groups', and each group contained a director, an animator and an assistant. As Willema Wong Tejeda (2005) points out, the system allowed for the interrelation of functions and the interchange of roles. This in turn supported stylistic diversity in the unit's productions.

HARRY READE JOINS ICAIC

ICAIC's successful emergence as a 'tool of the revolution' and its search for creative participants in the new animation department attracted Harry. Late in 1961, he presented himself to the members of Dibujos Animados ICAIC and screened his 16-mm copy of *Land of Australia: Aboriginal Art*. Hernán Henriquez recalled Reade's appearance at ICAIC:

> [It] looked as if *Tarzan* had stepped into my room—blond, blue eyes, completely dishevelled (like a lion with its mane) speaking some Spanish words in his 'Tarzan language'. In that moment, Harry looked like *Tarzan* coming from the jungle; an alien from planet Mars...with time [he] became one of the more interesting among the people I met...really very special...'El Canguro' (The Kangaroo). [His] first words were, 'I come from Australia because I hear there is a Revolution here and I am a revolutionary man, I came here to be part of this social project'.
>
> (*Henriquez, H. 2006b*, interview)

According to Henriquez, Reade explained that *Land of Australia: Aboriginal Art* was made using illustrations and rudimentary cinematic techniques, which created the effects of action. Its story was told without using the conventional process of animation. After convincingly demonstrating his ability as a director and cartoonist and stressing his commitment to the Revolution's ideology, Harry was offered a position as a director of animated films (Henriquez, H. 2006b, interview). He was then invited to submit a concept which reflected ICAIC's aim of serving the interests of both the new State and its people.

Reade conceived and drew the storyboard for his first project, *La Cosa* (*The Thing*, 1962). The narrative begins with the sudden appearance of a small lively bean-like 'thing' which soon attracts the attention of passing figures representing social institutions of commerce, science, the clergy and the military. The figures assess the value of the 'thing' with regard to their own particular interest but none can find a use for it. A peasant boy, however, recognises its value, plants it, nurtures it and the 'thing' grows into a tree which bears fruit (Figure 4.1).

La Cosa makes the audience aware that modern industrial society, as argued by Marx in *Das Kapital,* had changed the relationship between humankind and the world. Under capitalism, Marx contended that where everything is a product for sale, human lives, relationships and values become products with exchange values. This leads to dehumanisation such that workers, who are incorporated into the machinery of production, are alienated from the product of their labour. With *La Cosa*, Reade adopts Marx's method of seeking a more discerning way of seeing the realities of life. Thus the intention of the film is didactic. The organic bean 'thing', in *La Cosa*, is linked to common sense and the removal of an alienating element or gulf that estranges man from nature. The world view of capitalism where products confront workers as something natural and entirely separate from their makers was to Marx a false one, perpetuated to the political advantage of the wealthy ruling classes (Marx, K. 1997, 10).

FIGURE 4.1   Still frames from *La Cosa* (1962) conceived and directed by Harry Reade. (Courtesy of ICAIC.)

Reade's designs for the project extended the open line work drawing style he had developed in his press cartoons and incorporated characteristics of the emerging ICAIC style which was strongly influenced by UPA—simple figures, strong poses, limited animation and the absence of backgrounds or depth of field. The stylistic conventions of UPA displaced graphic realism and provided Reade with the symbolic means with which to convey Marx's concept of *alienation*. The style's rejection of naturalism *alienated* an audience from everyday reality so that their thoughts about that reality might be reinterpreted in a new light.

Hernán Henriquez, who was assigned as the project's animator, demonstrated his considerable skill in advancing the script through animated action rather than supportive dialogue. There was also strong character differentiation between the figures.

Interestingly, with its critique of capitalism, *La Cosa* was a great success with both Cuban and international audiences. The film achieved a significant place in Dibujos Animados ICAIC's history when it received Cuba's first international award for animation at the 1963 London Film Festival where it was considered to be one of the 'Outstanding Films of the Year'.

While promoting the image of the Revolution within Cuba and abroad, Dibujos Animados ICAIC also attracted the interest and attention of other nationally sponsored animation organisations. In 1964, notable animation luminary Norman McLaren, head of the National Film Board of Canada's (NFBC) Animation Department, undertook a cultural exchange visit to Estudios Cubanacan. The NFBC Animation Department's objective of 'making Canada familiar to Canadians and foreigners alike', endorsed the concept of public service and spirit of social concern present in ICAIC's priority of 'making movies that served the interests of both the new State and the people it presided over'. Henriquez said, McLaren sympathised with socialism and wanted to help developing countries produce their own animation (Zagury, L. 1999).

Following the international success of *La Cosa*, the relationship between Harry Reade and Jesús de Armas began to sour.

Juan Padrón believes that De Armas may have found it difficult that his department's efforts to project a form of Cuban expression to the international community had received its first distinction through the work of a foreigner (Padrón, J. 2006b, interview). Also, as director of Dibujos Animados ICAIC, De Armas had been responsible for nurturing the unit's creative and intellectual ethos. Considering De Armas' impressive body of work and his authoritative position, one wonders why there should have been conflict with Reade. One of ICAIC's founding members, cinematographer Harry Tanner, provided some perspective on the discord between the two. He suggests that Reade had deliberately begun to contest De Armas' authority:

> The differences in character and convictions between them were just insurmountable. Jesus was very surly and introspective, very sure that he was the greatest animator in the world. Harry, of course, would never agree. When he talked about De Armas he would say his name with an English pronunciation and made it sound like a swear word.
>
> (*Tanner, H. 2006*, interview)

All ICAIC members faced ideological challenges in their attempts to forge the new cultural politics of the Revolution through creative work. De Armas emphasised themes dealing with capitalism and Cuba's relationship with the United States. *La Prensa Seria* (*The Serious Press*, 1960) criticised private newspapers and advocated State control; *El tiburon y las* sardinas (*The Shark and the Sardines*, 1960) symbolised the conflict between imperialism and revolution; *El Cowboy* (*Cowboy*, 1962) satirised the hero figure of American westerns; *Remember Giron* (1961) illustrated Cuban success over US aggression at the Bay of Pigs; *The Burning of the Cane Field* (1961) dealt with terrorist acts perpetrated by US aeroplanes; and *Cuba Yes, Yankee No* (1963) dealt with the importance of literacy (Tejeda, W. W. 2005).

Although in the wake of the Bay of Pigs invasion Cuba's economic ties with the United States were severed, it was saved from economic collapse by the Soviet Union, which absorbed much of its sugar crop and provided imports. The ties established between Cuba and the Soviet Union imposed a communist orthodoxy in matters of politics and economics. When it came to questions of culture, however, it was a very different story. The Stalinist concept of socialist realism was widely considered to be irrelevant by Cuban artists who sought inspiration in avant-garde movements. Importantly, Alfredo Guevara successfully defended ICAIC's autonomy and its filmmakers' right to fulfil their artistic vocation, even when this meant taking a critical position. This included defending both the liberals who feared the encroachment of the State, and orthodox Marxists associated with the old guard of the Communist Party, who sought the application of socialist realism schemes. Many Cuban filmmakers had studied in Rome prior to the Revolution and through their work paid homage to Eisenstein and Fellini as well as the French New Wave and Brazilian Cinema Novo. Subsequently, Cuban cinema became identified not only with anti-imperialism but also with films in which 'the aesthetic of the European new wave is metamorphosed through a kind of revolutionary transfiguration'. ICAIC thus became a focus of opposition to any effort to impose aesthetic formulas like socialist realism on its cultural production (Chanan, M. 2004, 5–15). This apparent freedom from ideological control, however, was tempered by the dictum pronounced in Castro's 1961 speech, *The Words to the Intellectuals*. It encapsulated the Revolution's cultural position—'Within the Revolution, everything; against it, nothing' (Castro, F. 1972).

Padrón believed that Reade saw animation as a medium that could tell stories in a simple way and was opposed to indirect portrayal of themes utilising symbolism. This meant that his approach was contrary to the 'intellectual' Cuban directors who were inclined to use complex backgrounds, special camera movements and effects. Reade saw this approach as indulging in

experimental and avant-garde activity which resulted in complicated stories nobody understood (Padrón, J. 2006b, interview).
He took an orthodox Marxist stance and rejected representations
associated with bourgeois individualism. He promoted creative
work directed towards an audience that had suffered an intoler-
able reality under capitalist exploitation. His abrasive dismissal
of experimental projects exacerbated the antagonism with De
Armas. Harry Tanner felt that Reade's position was driven by his
understanding of socialist realism as 'culture for the masses …
Harry was always interested in the didactic use of cinema and he
saw a great need for that in Cuba' (Tanner, H. 2006, interview).

The ideological clash between De Armas and Reade illustrated
that 'Marxism' was a contested term, not one with a homogenous
body of doctrine with secure meaning and unity. It mirrored the
1921 debate between the Constructivists and Suprematists in
Russia when Soviet artists Rodchenko, Stepanova, Popova and
the Stenberg brothers felt obliged to question the role of art in
the new Soviet collective. They targeted the 'bourgeois individualism' expressed in the works of Suprematists Malevich and Tatlin
as being 'far from responding to the new political and economic
demands' of the Russian Revolution (Bois, Y. A. 1991, 101–102).

Reade was not a typical member of ICAIC's animation studio.
The contradiction between his individual stance and his desire
to support the collective was often exposed. Hernán Henriquez
remembered that his fierce sense of independence clashed with
De Armas' efforts to impose revolutionary zeal on studio members. De Armas demanded that ICAIC workers observe routine
working hours, but this was anathema to Reade who rejected rigid
work regimens or attempts by institutions to impose discipline
on him. His personal political viewpoint had been formed by his
experiences with his father and their life together on the road in
Australia. He held to the anarchist ethos of Lafargue's, *The Right
to be Lazy*. He scorned fellow workers who adhered to punctuality
or were told what to do. For colleagues like Henriquez, Reade's
behaviour was difficult to comprehend and at times offensive. On

one occasion, after arriving late, Reade shocked Henriquez by greeting him with, 'Hey, esclavo, te tienen ahi trabajando duro, eh? (*Hi, slave, they keep you working hard here, eh?*)'. Coming from a foreigner, such an insensitive comment was an insult to him and other Cubans who were shaking off the chains of colonial oppression (Henriquez, H. 2006b, interview).

Harry was not noted for his discipline or tact. Padrón claimed that as a director, he 'wrote his stories, made storyboards and character designs and then went fishing'. As a foreign volunteer assisting the Revolution, his excesses were tolerated with a leniency not granted to Cuban nationals. He regularly ignored militia orders given to do night guard-duty once a week and allowed his friends to cover for him (Padrón, J. 2004, interview). For him, 'slacking off' and letting others do his work had nothing to do with his commitment to Marxism. Reade acknowledges this contradiction in his unpublished manuscript. He suggests that his philosophy was not driven by selfishness, but rather by a distrust of social systems. He describes himself as 'one who could not lead, yet would not follow … an embittered cynical Caliban with glittering dreams'.[2] While he was prepared to answer 'the call' of revolution, he declared that he saw social institutions for what they were, 'a dreadful cage that held the human spirit captive—martyr to the jungle law' (Reade, H. 1998).

Despite Reade's contrary behaviour, Padrón, Tanner and Henriquez were adamant that his displays of independence, his creative talent and his freedom from fashionable artistic attitudes were admired by a core of ICAIC animators. This group was enthralled by his stories about life in Australia: the working class fighters of his time, union strikes, confrontations with police, brewing beer with bananas, bush cooking and how to cut hair with sheep shears. The stories made them feel that if all Australians were like Harry and they teamed up with Cubans, US Imperialism would be 'beaten to shit in a week' (Padrón, J. 2004, interview). However, Harry's collegiate support combined with his refusal to observe an imposed working regimen, threatened to shake Jesús de Armas' revolutionary rigour as well as his authority as director of the studio. De Armas resolved the growing conflict by offering Reade the opportunity to resign.

In 1963, Harry departed from ICAIC and joined the Instituto Cubano de Radiodifusion, ICR (TV) as an animation director. His first project accepted for production was *Viva papi! (Long live Daddy!)*, the tale of a boy who wishes his father had a more important job than just making nuts and bolts. He dreams of his father being a locomotive driver, a pilot flying a plane or a knight in armour. He learns, however, that if there were no nuts and bolts, the locomotive, the plane and the armour would fall apart and thus comes to appreciate the importance of his father's work. Like *La Cosa*, the intention of *Viva papi!* is didactic. Papi's seemingly insignificant labour advances the work and well-being of others. The voice-over and music for the project were provided by one of Cuba's most popular singers, Bola de Nieve.

When the project began and 16-year-old Juan Padrón was assigned to assist with the animation, Padrón's talent as a cartoonist and caricaturist had already been recognised by the Cuban magazines *Bohemia* and *Mella* and by 1963, he was producing a weekly cartoon strip page, called *El Hueco (The Hole)*, for the prestigious periodical *Mella* (Reloba, X. 2003).

Harry, however, was unhappy that an inexperienced teenager had been appointed to the project and demanded a more experienced animator. Management appeased Reade by engaging the studio's animation teacher Juan Jose Lopez as Padrón's supervisor. Lopez had left Barcelona in 1959 as a 20-year-old to escape Franco's fascist regime. In Havana, he was seconded by the Government to produce animation for the Comision de Orientacion Revolucionaria (COR) until it was disbanded in 1962 and he then worked briefly at ICAIC before taking a position at ICR (TV) training animators.

Reluctantly, Reade acceded to the studio's demand for Padrón to assist him because he considered Lopez to be the best animator in Cuba at the time and having him on the project was reassuring. Also, Lopez had mentored Padrón as a young cartoonist producing work for *Bohemia* and *Mella*. Padrón recalled the communication difficulties that followed:

> Juan [Lopez] is deaf, cannot hear and talks like a ventriloquist, so imagine me as a translator from one guy to the other. Harry didn't understand Juan's voice at all and Juan could not read Harry's lips with his heavy accented Spanish.
>
> (*Padrón, J. 2006b*, interview)

Progress on *Viva papi!* was slow. Juan received very few drawings to guide him and he struggled to interpret Reade's instructions which came in a mixture of Spanish and English:

> We made readings of the story, but I couldn't understand Harry one hundred percent. I [only] understood the film months afterward. He [was] always complaining he had a sixteen year old animator [and] shouting if I didn't copy exactly his designs. [He] used to come very slowly into the room trying to catch me away from my drawing table. After I gave him the idea of using Bola de Nieve for the voice and music, he didn't allow me to help further with the sound track. [He] invited me to celebrate the end of the film at the Havana Libre (old Hilton) and bought me a cheese sandwich.
>
> (*Padrón, J. 2006b*, interview)

Despite Harry's initial distrust of Padrón, and his attempts to impose his will on the production of *Viva papi!*, he and Juan developed a close friendship which according to Henriquez became 'uña y carne' (nail and flesh) (Henriquez, H. 2006a, interview). While Harry could be fiercely judgemental and confronting, he could also be charismatic and charming. He recognised and nurtured young raw talent and boosted the confidence of those he supported. Not only did he have a constructive impact on the young Juan but also on prominent ICAIC animator Tulio Raggi and illustrator Luis Lorenzo. 'He was a guru for us', said Juan Padrón.

> He taught me a lot about scriptwriting and the need to work hard in improving my drawings; to study classic novels and films; that culture is also learning to do things with your hands; to learn from the farmers and very poor people; to learn to call trees by their names, as he used to say. Also he was like a big brother or a father to me. He shared everything with his friends and taught us a lot. We had fun working together because he wanted to teach me to be the best.
>
> (*Padrón, J. 2004*, interview)

Harry Tanner said that Reade contributed significantly to Juan Padrón becoming Cuba's foremost animator/humourist and that other animators like Tulio Raggi respected him and regularly sought his advice (Tanner, H. 2006, interview). Padrón's subsequent career as an animator and cartoonist is well documented in animation histories. He is widely acknowledged as the premier Cuban animator of his generation having 'combined and balanced the requirements of culture and the need for entertainment in his vast productions, whilst providing leadership for Cuban animators' (Bendazzi, G. 1994, 387–388). A prolific artist, Padrón's extensive animation credits encompass more than 70 works including Cuba's first feature length animated film *Elpidio Valdés* (1979), followed in 1983 by *Elpidio Valdés contra dollar y cañn* (*Elpidio Valdés against guns and dollars*) and his most famous, *Vampires in Havana* (1985).

Interestingly in 1975, Juan's short film *La Silla* (*The Chair*, 1974) became the second Cuban film to win an international prize for animation when it received the Villa de Gijón prize at the International Festival of Cinema for Children at Girón, Spain. Harry's *La Cosa* having received the first one 12 years earlier. Both *La Silla* and *La Cosa* have educational themes that comment on the way humans interact with their world. *La Cosa* illustrates the importance of understanding and preserving nature, while *La Silla* focuses on the history of chairs and isolates the *school chair* as being the most important of all because it facilitates education, which in turn supports human development.

In 1982, Juan Padrón found a deteriorating 16-mm print of *Viva papi!*. Fearing that it could be lost to posterity and wishing to pay tribute to Harry's original concept and the music track of Bola de Nieve he decided to remake the film 'changing details here and there' (Padrón, J. 2006b, interview). Seven years later, *Viva papi!* was selected by the Cultural Council of the Cuban Institute of Cinema as one of its 30 best animated films.

EXHIBITING FILMS PRODUCED IN CUBA

Financial constraints and a sustained economic blockade by the United States made it almost impossible for Cuba to obtain movies from North America and other capitalist countries. Ironically, this had a positive effect on works produced by ICAIC. Fewer imports meant that home grown films enjoyed a larger share of the Cuban audience which in turn helped cinema to nourish social cohesion (Chanan, M. 2004, 33). As Juan Padrón explained:

[The Government] cut down film ticket prices to one peso per person so everybody could afford it. Films were exhibited in cinema theatres all over the island, showing a couple of newsreels, a cartoon, and then the feature film. ICAIC also made truck and boat travelling cinemas [Cinemóviles], showing films in the mountains to farmers, soldiers and students, and to the fishing fleet. They showed evening films five days a week on TV with specialists talking about cinema history and so on. As you see we were film crazy and you can be sure everybody saw your film.

(*Padrón, J.* 2004, interview)

The animated works produced by Reade in Cuba, therefore, were enjoyed by a large local constituency while his Australian work, on the other hand, had an audience limited to the WWF membership and a small number of metropolitan film festivals. Through his Cuban works he achieved his long cherished goal of producing art for the masses, a decision he made after rejecting fine art.

A BRIEF PERIOD IN MOSCOW: PERSONAL MATTERS

In 1963, Harry met and fell in love with Elga Efimova, a Russian woman who was working as a translator for the Cuban Academy of Science in Havana. On learning of Elga's apparent interest in Reade, her Bulgarian boy-friend got drunk and slapped her. When Harry found out he tracked him down and took him on in a fight which ended with the Bulgarian lying unconscious in a hotel lobby. Following the episode Reade was swept into a passionate relationship with Elga (Padrón, J. 2006b, interview). Hernán Henriquez described her as an intelligent, beautiful, statuesque young woman with a great deal of charisma. In Harry's company, she was like 'beauty and the beast—a beautiful exotic flower in the middle of a rough garden' (Henriquez, H. 2006b, interview) (Figure 4.2).

After several months, when Elga returned to Moscow, her departure immobilised Harry, who could not work but instead took to 'crying and drinking like a Mexican *charro*'.[3] In a smitten state, he persuaded the management of *Hoy* not only to obtain a visa for him to travel to the USSR but also to pay for his flight to Moscow where he and Elga married (Padrón, J. 2006b, interview). The newlyweds shared an apartment with Elga's mother and son Kolia from her first marriage. Reade found work illustrating Soviet children's magazines and books and producing cartoons

FIGURE 4.2   Elga Efimova and Harry Reade in Havana c.1963 (*above*), Juan Padrón and Harry Reade, Havana 1989 (*below*). (Courtesy of Juan Padrón and Pat Evans.)

for *Il Krokodil*, a satirical periodical for workers which was for published in Moscow. He also began translating Kruschev's biography and worked for the junior edition of *Pravda*, the leading Soviet Union newspaper and official organ of the Central Committee of the Communist Party (Evans, D. 2005, interview).

During 1964, after Harry's relationship with his mother-in-law became very strained, he Elga and Kolia returned to Havana where he resumed political cartooning with *Hoy*. He also did illustrations for the youth magazine *Pionero* and the satirical paper *Palante Y Palante*. Elga regained her position as a translator in the Information Centre at the Cuban Academy of Sciences (Padrón, J. 2006b, interview).

On his return to Cuba, Harry discovered that his nemesis Jesús de Armas had resigned his position as Director of Dibujos Animados ICAIC. With De Armas no longer in charge, the ideological direction of the studio had changed. Under him, it had been committed to experimentation, the search for distinctiveness in design, technique and styles of animation and exploration of narrative themes. The work produced reflected diverse influences and styles ranging from UPA, to the poetic atmosphere present in Czech puppet animation, to Polish symbolism used in cartoon and marionette films, through to the varied visual styles of avant-garde painting (Tejeda, W. W. 2005).

Under new direction Dibujos Animados ICAIC was fostering the production of didactic material which aligned with Reade's philosophy of reaching the working class rather than the intellectuals, and films being an 'educational tool for young people' (Padrón, J. 2004, interview). Proclaiming his desire to participate in the studio's new direction, Reade was reinstated as an animation director. The next two films that he wrote and directed affirmed his intention of utilising animation as an educational tool. The concept for the first, a 5-minute short, *El Arbol* (*The Tree*, 1967), was inspired by his environmental concerns and was aimed at peasant farmers. A cautionary tale about protecting nature from mankind, the film depicts a man negligently burning a tree that had offered him protection from the elements. When he later discovers the tree is sprouting, he nurtures it with much greater care. The animators for the film were Hernán Henriquez and José Reyes.

Reade's second educational film, *Microscopio El* (*The Microscope*, 1968, 4 minutes), was aimed at children and followed a father explaining a microscope to his son: how it is used, and how to make a rudimentary device based on the principles of light and lenses. José Reyes followed Reade's designs and direction to animate the film.

ICAIC's shift in aesthetic and ideological direction encouraged the development of didactic animated series. These lengthier projects relied upon the creation of national cartoon characters. A similar development occurred in East European countries where a strong commitment to socialist realism ideology led to the rejection of avant-garde movements. Rather than pursuing themes and styles considered bourgeois, animators from the region were urged to look for inspiration in folkloric and popular traditions— 'in ageless peasant songs or handed-down legends and tales' (Bendazzi, G. 1994, 163). Accordingly, ICAIC's new direction resulted in popular comic strip stories being adapted for animation. In 1966, Henriquez produced the series *Gugulandia*, which was based on an Afro-Cuban folk legend about a naïve caveman's understanding of the world around him. Throughout the 1970s, Juan Padrón extended his successful *Pionero* weekly children's magazine comic strip *Elpidio Valdes* into a humorous animated series. Valdes is a 'mambi', a nineteenth-century Cuban patriot, who revisits Cuba's struggle for independence from Spain, in the process offering Cuban children an historically accurate view of their ancestors' lives (Bendazzi, G. 1994, 387).

THE PEPE SERIES

In 1968, ICAIC cinematographer Harry Tanner was instructed by the head of the Documentaries Department to produce an instructional film showing how civilians could protect themselves in the event of an attack from American bombers. Believing that didactic themes could be communicated more effectively using humorous animation, Tanner sought Harry Reade's input:

> This was during the time of the war in Vietnam and the Cuban Civil Defence was impacted by how the Vietnamese were able to overcome the many bombings of their cities. I thought that the film would go over much better if the rather tragic theme had a few light moments. I had already worked with Harry in our first collaboration, *90 Millones*, where he created and animated a very humorous background for the titles. This film was shown in commercial cinemas many, many times and everybody would break out laughing at the titles. The theme of the documentary was to show the advances in the production of eggs in Cuba, the 90 million referring to the amount of eggs per year. At that time there was not too many other choices in proteins for consumption, so we all had many eggs in many forms.
>
> (*Tanner, H. 2006*, interview)

Reade responded by developing the urbane comic hero *Pepe* for the project. According to Hernan Henriquez, the character evolved from caricatures that fellow ICAIC animator Tulio Raggi drew of animator José 'Pepe' Reyes. Over time the studio staff had begun to see the drawings as an embodiment of the 'popular' Cuban man (Henriquez, H. 2006a, interview). Raggi and Reyes were engaged to animate the character, which provided comic relief from the serious matter of air-raid drills and the construction of shelters. The character also provided the film's title *Pepe Trinchera* (*Pepe Trench*) (Figure 4.3).

Pepe was well received by Cuban audiences and led to the development of three further films on which Reade directed the animation. Popular Cuban actor and cinema star Salvador Wood provided Pepe's character voice which addressed the audience in

FIGURE 4.3   Still frame of 'Pepe' from *Pepe cafetómano* (1968), conceived and designed by Harry Reade. (Courtesy of ICAIC.)

the Cuban vernacular. They identified with *Pepe* as he dealt with problems associated with agriculture, civic responsibility and health. Juan Padrón said that Cubans responded positively to the series because for the first time 'they could watch a cigar smoking mulato Cuban character in animation doing the same things and solving the same problems as themselves' (Padrón, J. 2004, interview). *Pepe cafetómano* (1968) explained how to grow coffee; *Pepe Voluntario* (1969) urged volunteers to overcome lethargy; and *Pepe Esparadrapo* (1969) illustrated how to apply first aid. Leonardo Piñero's animated sequences for all three episodes were integrated with live-action documentary footage.

Cinema historian Michael Chanan writes that post-1959 Cuban cinema engaged the audience by inviting viewers to become participants in the revolution they were observing. This was in stark contrast with offering entertainment that alienated viewers from

themselves and their social reality—as capitalist cinema some-
times did. Cuban cinema is a powerful instrument that helps
sustain social cohesion and offers outlets for social debate. He
stresses that:

> Politics in Cuban cinema is not a subtext that either the
> filmmaker or the critic can include or leave out: it is the
> inevitable ever-present inter-text of the aesthetic, and its
> constant dialogue with the political.
>
> (*Chanan, M. 2004*, 12)

Between 1968 and 1969, during production of the *Pepe* series,
Reade completed two more films. The first was *La Mentirita* (1969)
which was aimed at small children, warning them about the dangers of telling lies and how they can backfire on the perpetrator.
The film's message is conveyed through a young character who
invents a monster to scare his grandmother but ends up scaring
himself. José Reyes animated this two minute piece.

The second film *Dientes* (*Dental-health*, 1970, 4 minutes) was written and directed in collaboration with Tulio Raggi and animated by
Leonardo Piñero. It stressed the importance of dental hygiene.

DEPARTURE FROM CUBA AND ANIMATION

By 1969, Harry's interest in animation began to wane as he felt a
greater need to refine his writing skills. He began to eschew the
direct didactic approach to short animation projects in favour
of feature length live-action scripts. Tanner believed that after
Reade returned from the USSR, he grew tired of the antagonism
in ICAIC's Animation Department and wanted to follow a more
independent path. As time went on he was rarely seen at ICAIC
and because of his heated debates with other animators he was
being offered fewer projects. Tanner speculated that writing
offered Reade greater scope to deal with complex issues. He was
constantly searching for answers to his dilemmas and solutions
to his problems, and as he gained knowledge or experience of a

subject, he wanted to write about it. So, by the end of the 1960s he was writing rather drawing (Tanner, H. 2006, interview).

According to Juan Padrón, Reade was also struggling to reconcile his pro-Soviet sympathies with the stance of Castro's Revolutionary Government. He felt that Cuba was 'ungrateful' for the aid and support the Soviet Union had extended to the economy in the wake of the US embargo. He supported the Soviet Union's policy of 'diplomatic, non-guerrilla actions in Latin America', a view that was at odds with Che Guevara's pursuit of popular uprisings and armed overthrowing of capitalist regimes. He constantly argued over such topics with his friends and bosses and became increasingly provocative and obnoxious and prone to picking fights with men who stared at his beautiful wife. He also took delight in running the sidecar of his Soviet Ural motorcycle against old American cars parked in the avenues (Padrón, J. 2006b, interview).

> As far as animation was concerned, this creative period in his life was over. In 1969 he wanted to leave Cuba and find work as a writer in either Mexico or Canada. As a true believer, Elga would not contemplate leaving a socialist world or seeing her son raised under capitalism. Harry had his own priorities and became exasperated with Elga and her son, and his circle of friends. The small apartment became a 'hellhole' and the marriage collapsed. Elga returned to Moscow with Kolia and Harry was left with nothing: no wife, no child, no career, and no future.
>
> (*Tanner, H. 2006*, interview)

Late in 1969, Reade departed from Cuba and briefly worked as a journalist in Mexico where he reportedly lectured on intellectual freedom under socialism and capitalism with Ivan Illich— philosopher of the alternative society and author of *Deschooling Society*. The following year he headed to Canada, where he worked as a film reviewer and feature writer on the *Montreal*

Star and caught up with Harry Tanner who was visiting his hometown Toronto.

> [Harry] had come up north to make a new life. He came here thinking that at his age he was going to find work and sustenance because of his abilities. I argued saying that he was totally wrong, that he was trying to live a total dream that had no reality in the North America of the 70s. I suggested he should go back to Australia for there, at least, he knew the place. I said he was too old to make it here. He got a few really lousy jobs (unloading trucks in winter), but was able to find a room at the Langers (friends from Cuba) until they threw him out because of his increasing neurosis, and he left for Australia. I had returned to Cuba by that time and after that I never heard from him again. I only heard of him very rarely through Juan Padrón. I must confess that in spite of our arguments I missed him, for he had become part, sometimes an upsetting part, of my life.
>
> (*Tanner, H. 2006,* interview)

BACK TO WORK IN AUSTRALIA

In 1970, Harry returned to Australia where he worked as a journalist with the *Sunday Australian*. At the age of 53, he began writing plays. Within two years he had written five, three of which were workshopped at the 1982 National Playwrights Conference in Canberra.[4] His ambivalent view of life was presented in these works. Noted Australian dramatist Jack Hibberd wrote of the psychological themes Reade explored in one of his plays, *The Naked Gun*:

> This is ambiguity of the kind upon which the theatre thrives and survives. It is not artful and soulful obscurity. It is the awful lucid moment of sorting out

conflicting fates, conditioning against volition, the choosing of a life, the classical existential moment of decision making.

(*Hibberd, J. 1982*)

In 1984, Harry wrote and illustrated a children's book, *Whitefellers Are like Traffic Lights*, which promoted a message of tolerance and understanding among people of the world. In a follow-up publication titled *How Many Ropes on a Boat?*, he shared his nautical knowledge with children by explaining that every line, or 'sheet', on a boat has a different name and purpose.

After 40 years, the philosophical aim of the Studio of Realist Art continued to influence his creative activity. It underpinned his efforts to 'reveal social truths' and 'affirm the social value of art … by reacting directly to the world of experience' (Smith, B. 1945, 239–242).

CUBAN ACKNOWLEDGEMENT

In 1989 when ICAIC celebrated its 30 year anniversary, the animation department invited its founding members so it could acknowledge the important roles they had played in establishing the organisation and furthering the cultural interests of the Cuban people. Harry Reade travelled from Australia to participate in the festivities, be reunited with his colleagues and receive a diploma honouring his service. His visit also coincided with celebrations for the youth magazine *Pionero* which awarded him a medal for helping to establish the organisation and to acknowledge his cartooning contribution.

Reade's visit to Cuba coincided with the aftermath and reforms that led to the collapse of communism in Russia and Eastern Europe. Undaunted, Harry retained his undying faith in socialism, vehemently rejecting the Soviet's submission to fundamental reforms. Whereas in 1969, he had advocated Cuba's embrace of the Soviet socialist system, 20 years later he was urging Cuba to distance itself from a dramatically changed and deteriorated system.

He argued in favour of constant struggle and praised the social and political gains of the Cuban Revolution to which he had committed so much physical and creative energy. Reflecting on developments that had taken place during the 20 years of his absence, he declared that as revolutionaries Cubans had never disappointed him.

One workplace practice in particular that brought him great delight was the adoption by Cuban farmers of the Australian method of cutting and hauling sugar cane (corte australiano)— something he had proposed in his 1961 study document (Padrón, J. 2004, interview). He was also overjoyed to find that a monument, dedicated to Ethel and Julius Rosenberg, the first American citizens to be given the death sentence for espionage by a US civil court, had been erected in a small garden park on the corner of Paseo and Zappata Street, in Havana.

Post-Revolution Cuba sought to have its artists and others express revolutionary spirit through art. Juan Padrón, who began his animation career with Reade as one of his mentors, acknowledged Harry had a significant influence on him particularly in scriptwriting and design (Padrón, J. 2004. interview).

Friend and fellow ICAIC filmmaker, Harry Tanner, was convinced that Reade's laconic humour and his sense of wit, along with his influence on younger animators to be his major contribution to Cuban animation. Reflecting on the impact of Reade's legacy on his own life, he added:

> His influence was mostly to do with how I saw socialism, culture and its relation to people, and the fact that one can do many things if you set your mind to it. I could say that he reinforced many of the thoughts I had still unclear in my mind, and he helped to refocus them.
>
> (*Tanner, H. 2006,* interview)

In 1970, cartoonist and ICAIC animation teacher Juan José Fernández left Cuba and returned to Barcelona, where he began working for the Bruguera Publishing house. His series *SuperLópez,* first published in 1978, earned him fame as one of Spain's most notable comic strip artists. During this time he lost contact with Reade but then, almost 30 years after leaving Cuba, he introduced a cartoon figure named *Harry Reade* to the *SuperLópez* series Number 35.

The character is described as 'an idealist coming from an English speaking country, perhaps Australia … of robust features but with good feelings' (Fernández, J. L. 2004b), set somewhere in a fictitious Central African nation, Fernández (aka JAN) portrays *Harry Reade* as a rugged international aid worker providing unconditional assistance to refugees fleeing the abuses of the tyrant *Bokassa Massa*. The character introduces himself by declaring, 'We belong to the O.N.G. We help without worrying who we help. I am Harry Reade' (Fernández, J. L. 1999, No 35) (Figure 4.4).

> He's a reminder of friends I left in Cuba. I have fond memories of Harry. He had a very strong personality. He was big, tall, with a rough look…imposing, but at the same time he had the heart of a boy. I saw him in love with a very beautiful Russian with whom he lived for some years and he was very tender with her. The image I have is this—strong and sensitive. He was a good person.
>
> (*Fernández, J. L. 2004a,* interview)

ICAIC's acknowledgement of Harry Reade in 1989 testified to the value of his contribution to Cuban culture which had been achieved through creative works imbued with a political spirit. While he had briefly engaged with animation in Australia, he found in Cuba a dynamic ideological framework, a critical mass of fellow conspirators and a receptive society who welcomed the socialist animation script writer and his mission. Through his animated works in Cuba, Reade fully realised the power to communicate ideas to a mass audience; a process he had begun to explore in the Waterside Workers Federation Film Unit.

FIGURE 4.4 The character 'Harry Reade' depicted in *SuperLópez*: *La Guerra De Lady Arana*, No. 35 ed. by Juan José Fernández (aka JAN). (Courtesy of JAN.)

NOTES

1. *Maná* is God's liquid and sweet food falling from the sky. Procrastinators, who wait for it, die of hunger. The earth must be worked to produce food (Padrón, J. 2006a, email to author).
2. *'Caliban'* was the name of the half-man half-fish in Shakespeare's last play, *The Tempest*. An anagram for 'canibal', whose etymology comes from carib: Caribbean.
3. When asked to translate *charro*, Padron replied, 'A *charro* is a Mexican cowboy. The rich ones used very well-tailored & decorated dark suits with the classic big big hat or *sombrero mexicano*. Usually they rode with 2 revolvers at the hip like Cisco Kid -a famous Hollywood *charro*. The poor wear clothes like Speedy González' (Padrón, J. 2006a, email to author).
4. Reade, H. 1982b. *The Naked Gun*. Montmorency, Vic.: Yackandandah Playscripts, Reade, H. 1982a. *Buck's Night at Susy's Place*. Montmorency, Vic., Reade, H. 1981. *The Execution of Steele Rudd*. Accessed through University of Queensland, Fryer Library, Brisbane.

CHAPTER 5

Harry Reade's Legacy

On 7 May 1998, Harry Reade died on Nugra Farm near Girvan, New South Wales. As requested, one-half of his cremated remains were sprinkled around an apple tree on the farm, the remainder in the Rosenberg Memorial Park in Havana. His ashes were taken there by documentary filmmaker David Bradbury, who recorded Juan Padrón scattering them in the park to the tune of *Waltzing Matilda* played by Cuban saxophonist Francisco Sanchez. The scene was a sub-text in Bradbury's film *Fond Memories of Cuba* (Bradbury, D. 2002).

As an outsider who had enjoyed a peculiar combination of closeness to and distance from the communities in which he lived, the spreading of Harry's ashes signified the strength of his com-mitment to two different worlds. Paradoxically, his position in Australian and Cuban society was determined by the fact that he did not really belong to either. His beliefs and actions helped him attain a degree of freedom that allowed him to deviate from social norms. Unbound by conventional commitments, Harry spent his life negotiating the tensions between collective fulfilment and his more individualist, even anarchic impulses. In Australia, his anti-capitalist stance brought him into conflict with the dominant ideological system, while in Cuba, his anarchist streak prevented him from becoming fully committed to the demands of the new socialist order. He rejected the aspirations of the Menzies' middle-class who lived by the values and sentiments of the imagined 'Australian way of life', and at the same time, he was constrained by the practice of communist orthodoxies. Within the fibre of both systems, he was a loose cannon.

Even though Reade adhered to radical philosophies, his political and social ambivalences illustrate that while individuals may be caught up in dramatic world events or ideologies, they do not necessarily conform to the stereotypes that often populate historical accounts. As an individual, Harry never fitted neatly into a capitalist or a communist system because he was unable to completely sacrifice his individual inclinations for the common good. His life demonstrates the contradictions that can exist between the individual and society, and it is upon such countervailing fulcrums that he can be understood.

Throughout his life, Harry tried his hand at various forms of creative expression. Press cartooning enabled him to effectively connect with ordinary people and offered him a voice and a 'social lever' capable of educating audiences or asserting views that were counter to the prevailing political mood. He rejected fine art because he believed artistic experimentation and use of symbolic imagery were fraught with elitism and as such did not connect with the masses. He eschewed it in favour of the more publicly accessible union banners and murals and made a major contribution to the Sydney Wharfies' Mural.

Through his involvement with the WWFFU, he discovered animation which gave him the opportunity to apply his talents in illustration, cartooning and writing. The experience convinced him that animation was, indeed, a mass medium suited to the needs of education, social commentary and change. While the animated output of the WWFFU constitutes an extremely small part of Australian cultural history, it nonetheless played a role in articulating views opposed to the mainstream as well as initiating a brief but dramatic career in animation for Harry Reade. The

Unit's aim to 'consolidate the understanding of the use of film as a powerful propaganda weapon in the union's struggle for justice and social progress', demonstrated Art's capacity to stimulate debates about national concerns.

Harry's involvement with the WWFFU combined with all the other influences on his earlier life prepared him for the role he would play in Cuba. They propelled him to respond to Castro's appeal for international support for the 'Revolution'. While many in his Sydney Push circle were sympathetic with changes taking place in Cuba, Harry was the sole Australian to join the Brigada Internacional at the Bay of Pigs. Following this dramatic event, he then found a creative niche in Cuba that enabled him to make a significant contribution to a revolutionary society's transformation in remarkable times.

Had Harry remained in Australia, he would have achieved little in animation given that, with the termination of the work of the WWFFU in 1959, it is unlikely he would have sought employment as an animator in the commercially orientated industry that existed at the time. In revolutionary Cuba, he was able to express his ideological beliefs through the content of ICAIC's creative works and in doing so demonstrated animation's potential to serve an instructive social function. The international success of *La Cosa* placed him in a position of authority that later allowed him to put his own stamp on the animation produced at Dibujos Animados ICAIC. His didactic approach devoid of artistic pretension appealed to everyday people.

Harry's colleagues in both Australia and Cuba remembered him as a 'difficult' person; however, all agreed that he had considerable creative talent. While he remained the quintessential individualist and outsider, he succeeded in combining social commitment with cultural expression. The desire to communicate with an audience challenged him and, at times, forced him to conform to the expectations of the communities in which he lived. During these periods of constructive social interaction, Reade *did* collaborate with significant Australian and Cuban artists, and he *did* make valuable contributions to a broad range of artistic expression in both countries. His achievements in animation testify to the way in which a politically motivated artist can create beneficial social intersections.

From the Sydney waterfront to Havana, from Bob Menzies to Fidel Castro, Harry Reade's extraordinary life was a voyage of mind and body and a guide to the icons of a generation. His story provides an insight into broader historical events such as the Great Depression, the rise of communism and the Cold War and the Cuban Revolution, and the way a social realist animator was shaped by them. He applied writing and cartooning skills, ideological convictions and humour to his work, and in doing so brought a Marxist outlook to animation. It is significant that he achieved this during the Cold War period when there was vigorous community debate about what was the best society in which people should live. The Menzies' era goals of Cold War containment, uninterrupted economic growth and optimism were challenged by alternative voices such as that of Harry Reade who provoked people to think critically about their imagined communities. Although at times individuals may disagree with the aspirations of the majority, they can still make a worthy contribution to the nation's identity.

Reade recognised his own restlessness and inability to fully commit to social systems—an assessment that could equally be applied to his engagement with artistic expression:

> Looking back on it, my life has been a random shot carelessly fired … forever spanging and zinging away at wild tangents … forever seeking targets without reaching them or striking one squarely enough to become embedded.
>
> (*Reade, H. 1998*)

Throughout his life, Harry's character and convictions remained consistent. Although after returning to Australia in 1969, he continued to express himself through journalism, writing and children's book illustration, in the same vein, these works never had the same impact as those he had produced in Cuba. Paddy McGuiness believed that while Harry struggled with political and social ambivalences, he maintained his lifelong commitment to the dream of totalitarian socialism and granted special virtues to Cuba's communist regime despite the social hardship the country may have endured:

> He was impervious to argument or evidence. Indeed, in his later years he would, if challenged on the virtues of Stalin, the Cuban dictatorship, the guilt of the Rosenbergs or any other article of faith, simply burst into tears. This reflected his essential honesty and decency. He knew the dream stank, but could not abandon it.
>
> (*McGuinness, P. P. 2002*)

Harry's involvement with animation did not last long, but he achieved much with the medium in Cuba where his charismatic personality, his creative work, his laconic sense of humour and his influence on young Cuban animators, particularly Juan Padrón, left their mark. The themes of his animated films were both rational and poetic. He found a way to blend his belief system and self-taught creative skills into an effective whole. In doing so he brought his own voice to animation. The works he produced in Cuba are acknowledged as having had a major impact on the educational sector that helped shape the nation's social revolution.

Harry Reade did not acquire his Marxist convictions about the art of the working class by accident, but by participating in class struggles in the communities in which he lived. He placed his creative skills in the service of the working class who responded to his 'innate humour and ability to focus it on something affecting the world or its societies' (Tanner, H. 2006, interview). While the basic set of interests that informed his animation was acquired in Australia, the strong confluence of his interests in Cuba enabled him to fulfil his ambition to use art to help people in practical ways as well as engage large sectors of the population in discussion about the meaning and quality of their lives.

Appendix: Harry Reade's Filmography

Title:	**Land of Australia: Aboriginal Art**
Country of Origin:	Australia
Production Company:	Link Films/Waterside Workers' Federation of Australia Film Unit
Year of Production:	1956
Accessed:	National Film and Sound Archive (Australia)
Title No.:	16868
Category:	Animation
Language:	English
Colour:	Colour
Sound:	Sound
Gauge:	16 mm
Running Time:	9 minutes 45 seconds
Animation Director:	Reade, Harry; Millward, Clem
Animator	
Cinematography:	Gow, Keith; Levy, Jock; Disher, Norma
Editor:	Disher, Norma
Narrator:	Teale, Leonard
Copyright contact:	Waterside Workers' Federation of Australia

Synopsis: A short animated documentary highlighting Aboriginal culture and beliefs as represented through traditional art and creation legends. Two Aboriginal legends, 'Wyamba the Turtle' and 'Bohra the Kangaroo' are illustrated.

Title:	**Click Go the Shears**
Country of Origin:	Australia
Production Company:	Link Films
Year of Production:	1956
Accessed:	National Film and Sound Archive (Australia)
Title No:	15037
Category:	Animation
Language:	English
Colour:	Colour
Sound:	Sound
Gauge:	16 mm
Running Time:	5 minutes 17 seconds
Animator:	Reade, Harry
Producer:	Peter Hamilton
Cinematography:	Gow, Keith; Levy, Jock
Editor:	Disher, Norma
Narrator:	Teale, Leonard
Copyright contact:	Peter Hamilton

Synopsis: An animated cartoon illustrating the ballad, 'Click go the Shears'.

Original Title:	**Cosa, La**
Director:	Reade, Harry
Country of Origin:	Cuba
Production Company:	ICAIC
Year of Production:	1962
Category:	Animation
Language:	Spanish
Colour:	Colour

Sound:	Sound
Gauge:	35 mm
Length:	156 m
Running Time:	5 minutes 44 seconds
Concept:	Reade, Harry
Script:	Reade, Harry
Head of Production:	Prats, Paco
Design:	Reade, Harry
Backgrounds:	Reade, Harry
Animation:	Henriquez, Hernán
Animation Camera:	Rodriquez, Jose
Sound:	Guardia, Lucas de la
Editor:	Guardia, Lucas de la
Music Composition:	Gala, Natalio
Studio:	ICAIC
Distribution:	ICAIC

Synopsis: The value of a small bean-like 'thing' cannot be found by agents of commerce, science, the clergy and the military. Discarded, it is nurtured by a small peasant boy. It grows into a tree bearing fruit.

Note: Production details for **Viva papi!**, written and directed by Harry Reade and animated by Juan Padrón, are unavailable.

Original Title:	**Arbol, El**
Director:	Reade, Harry
Country of Origin:	Cuba
Production Company:	ICAIC
Year of Production:	1967
Category:	Animation
Language:	Spanish
Colour:	Colour
Sound:	Sound
Gauge:	35 mm
Length:	140 m
Running Time:	5 minutes

Concept:	Reade, Harry
Script:	Reade, Harry
Head of Production:	Prats, Paco
Design:	Reade, Harry
Backgrounds:	Reade, Harry
Animation:	Henriquez, Hernán; Reyes, José
Animation Camera:	Rodriquez, Pepin; Hernández, Adalberto
Sound:	Guardia, Lucas de la
Editor:	Guardia, Lucas de la
Music Composition:	Guerra, Armando
Narration:	Reade, Harry
Studio:	ICAIC
Distribution:	ICAIC

Synopsis: A man exposed to the rigours of the elements, discovers a tree that he protects. Through negligence he burns the tree. When he discovers a sprout, he begins to take care of the tree with greater care.

Original Title:	**Microscopio, El**
Director:	Reade, Harry
Country of Origin:	Cuba
Production Company:	ICAIC
Year of Production:	1968
Category:	Animation
Language:	Spanish
Colour:	B&W
Sound:	Sound
Gauge:	35 mm
Length:	99 m
Running Time:	4 minutes
Concept:	Reade, Harry
Script:	Reade, Harry
Head of Production:	Prats, Paco

Design:	Reade, Harry
Backgrounds:	Reade, Harry
Animation:	Reyes, José
Animation Camera:	Rodriquez, Pepin
Sound:	Guardia, Lucas de la
Editor:	Guardia, Lucas de la
Narration:	Reade, Harry
Studio:	ICAIC
Distribution:	ICAIC

Synopsis: A father explains what a microscope is to his son, how it is used and how to make a simple homemade microscope.

Original Title:	**Pepe Trinchera**
Director:	Tanner, Harry
Country of Origin:	Cuba
Production Company:	ICAIC
Year of Production:	1968
Category:	Animation
Language:	Spanish
Colour:	B&W
Sound:	Sound
Gauge:	35 mm
Length:	206 m
Running Time:	7 minutes
Concept:	Tanner, Harry
Script:	Tanner, Harry
Head of Production:	Pantín, Estrella; Prats, Paco
Design:	Reade, Harry; Raggi, Tulio
Backgrounds:	Reade, Harry
Animation:	Raggi, Tulio; Reyes, José
Animation Camera:	Rodriquez, Pepin
Sound:	Guardia, Lucas de la
Editor:	Guardia, Lucas de la
Music Composition:	Guerra, Armando

Narration:	Tanner, Harry
Design of Credits:	Avila, René
Studio:	ICAIC
Distribution:	ICAIC

Synopsis: Due to the danger of an aerial attack, each citizen must know how to construct a refuge or dig a trench.

Original Title:	**Pepe Cafetómano**
Director:	Reade, Harry
Country of Origin:	Cuba
Production Company:	ICAIC
Year of Production:	1968
Category:	Animation
Language:	Spanish
Colour:	Colour
Sound:	Sound
Gauge:	35 mm
Length:	114 m
Running Time:	4 minutes
Concept:	Reade, Harry
Script:	Reade, Harry
Head of Production:	Prats, Paco
Design:	Reade, Harry; Villar, Carlos
Backgrounds:	Reade, Harry; Villar, Carlos
Animation:	Piñero, Leonardo
Animation Camera:	Rodriquez, Pepin
Sound:	Guardia, Lucas de la; Gálvez, Idalberto
Editor:	Guardia, Lucas de la
Music Composition:	Guerra, Armando
Narration:	Reade, Harry
Studio:	ICAIC
Distribution:	ICAIC

Synopsis: In a simple way, Pepe explains the processing of coffee.

Original Title:	**Mentirita, La**
Director:	Reade, Harry
Country of Origin:	Cuba
Production Company:	ICAIC
Year of Production:	1969
Category:	Animation
Language:	Spanish
Colour:	Colour
Sound:	Sound
Gauge:	35 mm
Length:	53 m
Running Time:	2 minutes
Concept:	Reade, Harry
Script:	Reade, Harry
Head of Production:	Prats, Paco
Design:	Reade, Harry
Backgrounds:	Reade, Harry
Animation:	Reyes, José
Animation Camera:	Rodriquez, Pepin
Sound:	Guardia, Lucas de la
Editor:	Guardia, Lucas de la
Music Composition:	González Giralt, René
Narration:	Reade, Harry
Studio:	ICAIC
Distribution:	ICAIC

Synopsis: The story attempts to teach children that lies are not good. A child invents a monster to scare its grandmother but ends up being scared itself.

Original Title:	**Pepe Voluntario**
Director:	Reade, Harry
Country of Origin:	Cuba

Production Company:	ICAIC
Year of Production:	1969
Category:	Animation
Language:	Spanish
Colour:	B&W
Sound:	Sound
Gauge:	35 mm
Length:	159 m
Running Time:	5 minutes
Concept:	Reade, Harry
Script:	Reade, Harry
Head of Production:	Prats, Paco
Design:	Reade, Harry
Backgrounds:	Martinez, José
Animation:	Piñero, Leonardo
Animation Camera:	Rodriquez, Pepin
Sound:	Guardia, Lucas de la
Editor:	Guardia, Lucas de la
Design of Credits:	Villar, Carlos
Narration:	Reade, Harry
Studio:	ICAIC
Distribution:	ICAIC

Synopsis: A humorous representation of the 'wings of vicissitude'. A character has an interest in voluntary work but is incapable of rising early.

Original Title:	**Pepe Esparadrapo**
Director:	Reade, Harry
Country of Origin:	Cuba
Production Company:	ICAIC
Year of Production:	1969
Category:	Animation
Language:	Spanish
Colour:	Colour

Sound:	Sound
Gauge:	35 mm
Length:	160 m
Running Time:	6 min
Concept:	Reade, Harry
Script:	Reade, Harry
Head of Production:	Prats, Paco
Design:	Reade, Harry
Backgrounds:	Reade, Harry
Animation:	Piñero, Leonardo
Animation Camera:	Rodriquez, Pepin
Sound:	Guardia, Lucas de la
Editor:	Guardia, Lucas de la
Narration:	Reade, Harry
Design of Credits:	Avila, René
Studio:	ICAIC
Distribution:	ICAIC

Synopsis: A humorous didactic film that teaches elementary first aid.

Original Title:	**Dientes**
Director:	Raggi, Tulio; Reade, Harry
Country of Origin:	Cuba
Production Company:	ICAIC
Year of Production:	1970
Category:	Animation
Language:	Spanish
Colour:	B&W
Sound:	Sound
Gauge:	35 mm
Length:	133 m
Running Time:	4 minutes
Concept:	Raggi, Tulio; Reade, Harry
Script:	Raggi, Tulio; Reade, Harry

Head of Production:	Rivas, Mario
Design:	Raggi, Tulio
Photography:	Maynulet, Gustavo
Animation:	Piñero, Leonardo
Animation Camera:	Rodriquez, Pepin
Sound:	Guardia, Lucas de la
Editor:	Guardia, Lucas de la
Narration:	Raggi, Tulio
Studio:	ICAIC
Distribution:	ICAIC

Synopsis: A film that explains the dangers of poor dental hygiene.

References

Agramonte, A. 1996. Cronología del Cine Cubano. Havana: Ediciones ICAIC.

Alfonso, C. 1962. Harry Reade Y Sus Dibujos (Harry Reade and his drawings). Hoy, 1 April, 1962.

ASIO. File on Henry Garbutt Reade. ASIO, Series: A16119, Item 1334.

Baker, A. J. 1975. Sydney Libertarianism & the Push. Broadsheet (No. 81, March).

Bannah, M. 1997. Meeting our man in Havana. Queensland Animators' Newsletter, No. 10.

Beasley, M. 1996. The wharfies: a history of the Waterside Workers' Federation of Australia. Rushcutters Bay, Sydney: Halstead Press in association with the Australian National Maritime Museum.

Bendazzi, G. 1994. Cartoons: one hundred years of cinema animation. Bloomington, Ind: Indiana University Press.

Bertrand, I. ed. 1989. Cinema in Australia: a documentary history. Sydney: New South Wales University Press.

Bois, Y. A. 1991. Material utopias. Art in America, Vol. 79, No. 5, June 1991, pp. 101–102.

Bolton, G. C. 1974. 1939–1951. In a new history of Australia, ed. Crowley, F. Melbourne: William Heinemann.

Bradbury, D. 2002. Fond memories of Cuba. Produced by Bradbury, D. and Rubbo, M. Australia: Ronan Films.

Bradbury, K. 1998. An ambivalent industry: how Australian animation developed. Thesis (M.A.). University of Queensland.

Bradbury, K. 2001. Australian and New Zealand animation. In Animation in Asia and the Pacific, ed. Lent, J. A. 207–222. Eastleigh, United Kingdom: John Libbey Publishing.

Burn, I., Lendon, N., Merewether, C. and Stephen, A. 1987. The necessity of Australian art: an essay about interpretation. Sydney: The University of Sydney Printing Service.

Burton, J. 1997. Film and revolution in Cuba. The first twenty-five years. In New Latin American cinema, Vol. 2 ed. Martin, M. T. Detroit: Wayne UP.

Caban, G. 1983. A fine line: a history of Australian commercial art. Sydney: Hale & Iremonger.

Castro, F. 1972. Words to the intellectuals. In Radical perspectives in the arts, ed. Baxandall, L. Harmondsworth: Penguin.

Chanan, M. 2004. Cuban cinema. Minneapolis; London: University of Minnesota Press.

Clark, C. M. H. 1987. A history of Australia: the old dead tree and the young green tree 1916-1935 with an epilogue. Carlton: Melbourne University Press.

Clark, D. 1981. A closed book? The debate on causes. In The wasted years, ed. Mackinolty, J. 10–26. Sydney: George Allen and Unwin.

Cobas, R. 1984. Notas para una cronologia del dibujo animado cubano. Cine Cubano, (110).

Day, D. 1998. The demise of the digger: Australian identity in a post-colonial world. In Australian identities, ed. Day, D. Melbourne: Australian Scholarly Publishing.

Dermody, S. and Jacka, E. 1987. The screening of Australia: anatomy of a film industry. Sydney: Currency Press.

Disher, N. 2005, 23 April. Interview with author.

Eisenstein, S. 1930. Soviet cinema. In Voices of October, New York.

Elliott, B. 1979. The Jindyworobaks. St Lucia: University of Queensland Press.

Evans, D. 2005, 11 April. Interview with author.

Evans, P. 2005, 11 April. Interview with author.

Fahey, W. 2004. Socialist folk singer set Lawson to music. The Sydney Morning Herald, 6 Feb 2004.

Farrell, F. 1981. International socialism & Australian labour: the left in Australia 1919-1939. Sydney: Hale & Ironmonger.

Fernández, J. L. 1999. SuperLopez: La Guerra De Lady Arana. No. 35 ed. Barcelona: Ediciones B, Grupo Zeta.

Fernández, J. L. 2004a, 16 March. Interview with author.

Fernández, J. L. 2004b. Ediciones B La Página Escarolitrópica Gmnésica De Superlópez.

Fitzgerald, R. 1984. From 1915 to the early 1980s: a history of Queensland. St. Lucia, Brisbane: University of Queensland Press.

Franklin, J. 1953. The push and critical drinkers. In Corrupting the youth: a history of philosophy in Australia, Paddington. NSW: Macleay Press.

Furniss, M. 1998. Art in motion: animation aesthetics. London: John Libbey.

General Reviews. 1958. Federation News (Bulletin of the Victorian Federation of Film Societies), 3.5.

Green, G. 1996. Rebel red puts ashore at Noosa with tales of Cuba. Courier-Mail, May 20, 1996.

Griffen, J. 1988. From Cuba to Glebe. Australian Listener, 19.

Gunzburg, D. 1996. Rebel Twilight. Produced by Gunzburg, D. for "Australian Story": Australian Broadcasting Commission. Artarmon, Sydney.

Haese, R. 1982. Modern Australian art. New York: Alpine Fine Arts Collection, Ltd.

Harrison, K. 1980. The points system for Australian content: a study in symbolic policy. Brisbane: Royal Institute of Public Administration.

Henriquez, H. 2006a, 25 January. Interview with author.

Henriquez, H. 2006b, 22 January. Interview with author.

Hibberd, J.1982. The naked gun, ed. Reade, H. Montmorency, Vic: Yackandandah Playscripts.

Horrocks, R. 2001. Len Lye: a biography. 2nd ed. Auckland: Auckland University Press.

Ingamells, R. 1938. Conditional culture. Adelaide: F.W. Preece.

Jolliffe, A. 2005, 7 April. Interview with author.

Keeble, A. 2001. In the spirit of wandering teachers. Melbourne: Ocean Press.

Klein, N. M. 1993. Seven minutes: the life and death of the American animated cartoon. London, New York: Verso.

Lafargue, P. 1883. Lafargue Internet Archive (marxists.org) 2000 The Right to be Lazy. https://www.marxists.org/archive/lafargue/1883/lazy/ (accessed 6 December, 2005)

Lendvai, E. 1998. Animated Cartoons in Hungary. http://www.filmkultura.hu/articles/essays/anim.en.html (accessed 10 February, 2006)

Lent, J. A. 2002. Animation World Magazine. Vampires, Lice and a Dose of History: Juan Padron and Cuban Animation. http://mag.awn.com/?article_no=1292 (accessed 6 January, 2006)

Levy, J. (NBAC/ANU, WWF, E211/163) 1957, 4 April. Letter to John Heyer.

Levy, J. 2005, 27 June. Interview with author.

Mallory, G. 1992. The social responsibility of labour. Oral History Association of Australia, Journal, Vol. 14.

Marx, K.1970. A contribution to the critique of political economy, ed. Dobb, M. New York: International Publishers.

Marx, K. 1997. Capital. In The Marx reader, ed. Pierson, C. Cambridge: Polity Press.

McGuinness, P. 2005, 11 April. Interview with author.

McGuinness, P. P. 2002. The revolution whose values vanished in a puff of cigar smoke. Sydney Morning Herald.

McQueen, H. 2004. Social sketches of Australia 1888-2001. 3rd ed. St Lucia, Queensland: University of Queensland Press.

Mendham, T. and Hepper, K. 1978. Special report: animation in Australia. In Industrial and commercial photography 1978 yearbook, 51–74. Sydney: Publicity Press.

Millward, C. 2005, 28 April. Interview with author.

Milner, L. 2003. Fighting films: a history of the waterside Workers' Federation film unit. North Melbourne, Vic: Pluto Press.

Monahan, C. 1989. Animated. Australia: Ronan Films.

Murphy, J. 2000. Imagining the fifties: private sentiment and political culture in Menzies' Australia. Sydney: Pluto Press.

Padrón, J. 2004, 13 October. Interview with author.

Padrón, J. 2006a, 20 September. Email to author.

Padrón, J. 2006b, 16 January. Interview with author.

Palmer, V. 1950. Old Australian Bush Ballads.

Petty, B. 2005, 31 May. Interview with author.

Reade, H. 1953. Reade between the Lines. Challenge, January 28, 1953.

Reade, H. 1961. Cartoonist helps Cuba. Tribune, July 26, 1961. p. 7.

Reade, H. 1981. The execution of Steele Rudd. Brisbane: University of Queensland, Fryer Library.

Reade, H. 1982a. Buck's night at Susy's place. Montmorency, Vic.

Reade, H. 1982b. The naked gun. Montmorency, Vic: Yackandandah Playscripts.

Reade, H. 1987. An elephant charging my chookhouse. Frenchs Forest, N.S.W., Lilyfield.

Reade, H. 1998. A funny kind of leftwing animal. Unpublished manuscript in Harry Reade's estate held in trust by Patricia Evans.

Reeves, A. 1991–1992. The Sydney Wharfies' mural. Museums Australia Journal, Vols. 2-3, 195–203.

Reeves, A. 1992. A tapestry of Australia: the Sydney wharfies mural. Sydney: Waterside Workers Federation, Sydney Port.

Reloba, X. 2003. Habanera #28 Juan Padrón: Behind Elpido's back. http://www.walterlippmann.com/docs298.html (accessed 6 January, 2006)

Roach, T. 1956. Report on Films. WWF Federal Council meeting minutes. 12 Oct. 1956. NBAC/ANU, WWF, E211/163.

Ross, E. 1982. Of storm and struggle: pages from labour history. Sydney: Alternative/New Age.

Schroeder, P. A. 2002. Tomás Gutiérrez Alea: the dialectics of a film-maker. New York, London: Routledge.

Smith, B. 1945. Place, taste and tradition: a study of Australian art since 1788. Sydney: Ure Smith.

SORA Bulletin. 1945. SORA Bulletin, (1).

Stephens, T. 1987. Harry's war with Fidel and Che. The Sydney Morning Herald: Saturday Review. 15 August, 1987, 45.

Stitt, A. 2005, 30 May. Interview with author.

Stock, A. M. 2009. On location in Cuba: Street filmmaking during times of transition. University of North Carolina Press.

Symons, B., A. Wells and S. Mcintyre 1994. Communism in Australia: a resource bibliography. Sydney: National Library of Australia.

Tanner, H. 2006, 20 March. Interview with author.

Tejeda, W. W. 2005. Miradas revista del audiovisual Cuban Animation: With both sides of history. http://www.miradas.eictv.co.cu/index.php?option=com_content&task=view&id=397&Itemid=81&lang =es (accessed 16 January, 2006)

Tribune. 1961a. Cuban films. Tribune, 22 November.

Tribune. 1961b. Wanted: a million pencils for Cuba. Tribune, 12 July.

Turner, I. 1965. Industrial labour and politics. Canberra: Australian National University.

Springwood Festival Camp. 1950. Walker, J. Produced by (Australia), R. F. U. Australia: Screen Sound Australia—National Screen and Sound Archive. [Film/documentary: 16 mm].

Waterhouse, R. 1995. Consensus and conformity: the fifties and beyond. In Private pleasure, public leisure: a history of Australian popular culture since 1788, South Melbourne: Longman.

Wharfie Film Unit Powerful Aid to Union Struggle. 1956. Maritime Worker, 6 March.

Williams, R. 1988. The politics of the avant-garde. In Visions and blue-prints: avant-garde culture and radical politics in early twentieth-century Europe, eds. Timms, E. and Collier, P. 2–14. Manchester: Manchester University Press.

Zagury, L. 1999. Animation World Magazine. A Chat with Hernán Henriquez. http://mag.awn.com/?article_no=1267 (accessed 6 January, 2006)

Index

Page numbers in *italics* refer to figures.

Milton Keynes UK
Ingram Content Group UK Ltd.
UKHW031534071024
449327UK00005B/42

9 780367 639532